1 0 1
Snappy Fashions

1 0 1
Snappy Fashions

Oodles of One-Piece Designs for Babies

Cathie Filian

LARK BOOKS

A Division of Sterling Publishing Co., Inc.
New York / London

Editor: Linda Kopp
Editorial Assistance: Amanda Carestio
Art Director: Kristi Pfeffer
Figurative Illustrations: Beth Sweet
Technical Illustrations: Orrin Lundgren
Baby Photography: Lynne Harty
Project Photography: Steve Mann
Cover Designer: Celia Naranjo

Library of Congress Cataloging-in-Publication Data

Filian, Cathie, 1970-
  101 snappy fashions : oodles of one-piece designs for babies / Cathie Filian. -- 1st ed.
    p. cm.
  Includes index.
  ISBN 978-1-60059-494-6 (pb-trade pbk. : alk. paper)
  1. Infants' clothing. 2. Fancy work. I. Title. II. Title: One hundred and one snappy
fashions.
  TT637.F56 2010
  646.4'06--dc22

                                        2009024456

10 9 8 7 6 5 4 3 2

Published by Lark Books, A Division of
Sterling Publishing Co., Inc.
387 Park Avenue South, New York, NY 10016

Text © 2010, Cathie Filian
Photography © 2010, Lark Books, a Division of Sterling Publishing Co., Inc., unless
otherwise specified
Illustrations © 2010, Lark Books, a Division of Sterling Publishing Co., Inc., unless
otherwise specified

Distributed in Canada by Sterling Publishing,
c/o Canadian Manda Group, 165 Dufferin Street
Toronto, Ontario, Canada M6K 3H6

Distributed in the United Kingdom by GMC Distribution Services,
Castle Place, 166 High Street, Lewes, East Sussex, England BN7 1XU

Distributed in Australia by Capricorn Link (Australia) Pty Ltd.,
P.O. Box 704, Windsor, NSW 2756 Australia

If you have questions or comments about this book, please contact:
Lark Books
67 Broadway
Asheville, NC 28801
828-253-0467

Manufactured in China

ISBN 13: 978-1-60059-494-6

For information about custom editions, special sales, premium and corporate
purchases, please contact Sterling Special Sales Department at 800-805-5489 or
specialsales@sterlingpub.com.

Contents

Introduction

Everywhere you turn, gossip and fashion magazines feature cutting-edge baby clothes worn by celebrity offspring. While Angelina, Nicole, and Tori can afford the hottest trendy looks from chic baby boutiques, most parents can't (or won't!) spend a fortune dressing a baby. But this doesn't mean that your shining star can't wear the coolest baby clothes around.

Just start with a plain snapsuit—or bodysuit or creeper or romper, depending on the term you use—which costs less than most of those gossip magazines. With a little creativity, you can design a look that is hip, easy on the wallet, and ready for a spin on any baby fashion runway.

This book contains more than 100 embellishing and design techniques for creating your own colorful styles. You'll also find simple ideas on how to throw a baby shower!

To make it even easier, the designs are categorized by technique. Chapters include ideas for dyeing, painting, appliqué, embroidery, and using ribbons and trims. You'll learn about iron-ons, patches, and how to create with cut, ripped, and torn elements. And don't forget to bring on the bling, or get baby decked out for the holidays.

Every chapter features 10 different original designs, each with a new technique to learn or explore and variation ideas to try. Don't worry if you're a beginner. Detailed instructions for all the techniques, as well as basic information and special tips will help you get fabulous results the first time around.

If you need ideas for celebrating the birth of a baby with style and flair, skip to Chapter 11. From baby-shower basics to templates for making your own party invites and decorations—it's all there, and it's all good. You'll also find out how to set up an embellishing station so partygoers can make on-the-spot gifts (cute snapsuits, of course). Even first-time hostesses will have no trouble throwing a memorable event.

I had fun creating the different designs, and I know you'll have as much fun making them. Once you feel confident, I hope the projects will inspire you to try your own designs. So forget about those plain snapsuits. It's time for baby to step into the spotlight while you let your imagination run wild.

Make It Snappy!

I know you're ready to dive in and start creating your first design, but there are a few basics you should know before you begin channeling your inner fashion designer.

Types of Snapsuits

Snapsuits are available in short sleeve or long sleeve and are generally 100 percent cotton. Because they're almost as necessary as diapers, manufacturers price them right; a snapsuit costs way less than a latté. You can also find them in value packs for even greater savings. If you want to invest a little more money, look for suits that are made from organic cotton, bamboo, or even hemp. All the designs in this book were made with white, 100 percent cotton suits and come from a variety of manufactures and retail stores.

Sizing

Snapsuits are sized according to the age of the baby. You can purchase packaged suits as small as newborn and as large as 3 toddler. Most snapsuits will have a weight and height chart on the back of the package or on the tag. For general sizing have a peek at the size chart on page 9.

Getting Started

You don't need much to get started creating custom outfits. All you really need to do is choose a design or technique, gather the materials needed, do a little prep work, and start creating.

Prepping a Snapsuit

Remove any sizing on the fabric and preshrink the suit by washing it in warm water with no fabric softener, and then dry it on medium. Don't skip this step. Fabric dyes, paints, iron-ons, fusible webbing, and fabric glue have a hard time sticking to sizing.

Basic Materials

You can embellish suits with anything from paints and iron-ons to embroidery floss and scrap fabrics. Each chapter in this book features a different technique. In the beginning of the chapter you'll find a detailed list of items you might need for that particular technique as well as basic techniques and tips.

Safety First

When embellishing a snapsuit, you want to make sure everything will be safe and comfortable for the little one. Embellishments such as buttons, rhinestones, or pom-poms should be small and securely attached to avoid a choking hazard. Avoid using rough and heavy fabrics. Instead, choose lighter weight, soft fabrics that won't scratch the baby's skin. Make sure to cut all dangling threads so tiny fingers don't get twisted in them.

Caring for Embellished Snapsuits

For most of the projects in this book, machine laundering is fine, but for some designs you might want to hand wash and hang dry. If you're using iron-ons or fabric paints, refer to the manufacturer's instructions for laundering. For dyed designs, be sure to wash with like colors.

That's it! Ready to begin?

AGE	WEIGHT	HEIGHT
Newborn	5–8 pounds (2.3–3.6 kg)	17–21 inches (43.2–53.3 cm)
0–3 Months	8–12 pounds (3.6–5.4 kg)	21–24 inches (53.3–61cm)
3–6 Months	12–16 pounds (5.4–7.2 kg)	24–27 inches (61–68.6 cm)
6–9 Months	16–18 pounds (7.2–8.2 kg)	27–28 inches (68.6–71.1cm)
12 Months	18–24 pounds (8.2–10.9 kg)	28–30 inches (71.1–76.2 cm)
18 Months	24–28 pounds (10.9–12.7 kg)	30–32 inches (76.2–81.2 cm)
24 Months	28–32 pounds (12.7–14.5 kg)	32–34 inches (81.2–86.3 cm)
3 Toddler	32–35 pounds (14.5–15.9 kg)	34–38 inches (86.3–96.5 cm)

Chapter 1
Dyeing

If you close your eyes and imagine every color in the rainbow or every hue in an art history book, then you'll be able to imagine all the different colors you can dye a snapsuit. And you don't have to settle for the color on the dye box; fabric dyes can be blended, brewed strong, or diluted with water to create thousands of different colors and tones.

If you're looking for color inspiration, think about other embellishments that you could use. Planning on attaching a patch or appliqué made from an old T-shirt? Choose a complementary dye color. Creating a holiday snapsuit? Choose colors that fit the season. When I'm stumped for a color palette, I look at greeting cards, stationery, scrapbook paper, wrapping paper, magazines, catalogs, and books.

Types of Dyes

Fabric dyes can be purchased online, at art supply stores, fabrics shops, and craft stores. For the home crafter or beginning dyer, there are only three varieties of fabric dye you need to worry about: fiber-reactive, acid, and all-purpose.

Fiber-reactive dyes are cold-water dyes that work best on cellulose fabrics or fabrics made from plants such as cotton, bamboo, linen, hemp, and rayon.

Acid dyes are hot-water dyes that are perfect for dyeing protein fabrics or fabrics that are from an animal, such as silk or wool.

All-purpose dyes are also hot-water dyes, but they have additives that allow them to work for both cellulose and protein fibers. They are commonly sold at grocery stores in the detergent section. This dye is great for a quick dye job, but I prefer fiber-reactive dyes.

Because the snapsuits I used for this book are all cotton, I used permanent, cold-water, fiber-reactive dye that holds color well.

Dyeing 101

Warning! This process is simple, but addictive. Once you've learned a few simple steps, I know you'll be dyeing snapsuits and all sorts of other clothing items as well.

Prepping the Snapsuit

Before mixing the dye, you need to prep the snapsuit. For best results, always use one made of 100 percent cotton. Prewash it to remove starch and sizing from the fabric's surface, but don't use liquid fabric softener or dryer sheets.

Next, evenly wet the suit. You don't want the fabric dripping wet, so wring it out if necessary. I always place mine in a plastic grocery bag while I'm preparing a dye bath. This prevents small dye particles from landing on the wet fabric, which can leave unwanted dye spots.

Step-by-Step Dyeing

Now you're ready for business! For best results, always follow the instructions on the dye package. I like to dye snapsuits in a large glass bowl. You want the fabric to float around freely in the dye bath, so make sure the bowl is wide enough. You can also dye in a plastic bucket or stainless steel sink.

WHAT YOU NEED
> Small glass bowl
> 1 package of dye
> 4 cups (1 L) of warm water
> Large glass bowl
> 4 teaspoons (20 g) table salt
> Rubber gloves
> Wooden spoon

WHAT YOU DO
In the small glass bowl, dissolve the dye in the 4 cups (1 L) of warm water, stirring thoroughly.

Fill the large bowl with warm water, leaving enough room to add the dye mixed in step 1. Add the salt to dissolve.

Add the dye mixed in step 1 to the salted water. Place the snapsuit in the dye bath. Stir for 15 minutes. Soak for 45 minutes or until the desired color is reached.

Rinse the suit in cold water until all the excess dye is removed. A good technique is to place it under running water until the water runs clear.

Carefully wring or roll the suit in a rag or towel to remove any excess water, and hang to dry. Wash as usual.

Working with Colors

By mixing colors, you can create your own signature shades. All you need to do is follow the principles of the color wheel: red and blue make purple, blue and yellow make green, and so on. To test your colors as you mix them, just dip a white paper towel into the dye bath.

If you want to create a lighter shade of a color, use a smaller amount of dye with the same amount of water. Of course, you'll still need to add 4 teaspoons (20 g) of salt.

For an intense, deep color, I use a smaller amount of salted water and keep the snapsuit in the dye bath for the entire 45 minutes.

Making Four (or More) Colors with One Packet of Dye

This simple trick will stretch your dye budget. By using this technique, you'll be able to get at least four different shades of a color from one dye packet.

WHAT YOU NEED
- 10 cups (2.4 L) of warm water
- 1 package of dye
- 8 teaspoons (40 g) of table salt
- 2 large glass bowls
- 1 cup (.25 L) measuring scoop
- Rubber gloves
- Wooden spoon

WHAT YOU DO

For the *darkest* color, mix the 10 cups (2.4 L) of warm water, 4 teaspoons (20 g) of salt, and dye in a large glass bowl. Stir until all the dye is dissolved.

To create the *lightest* color, fill the second glass bowl with warm water, and add the remaining 4 teaspoons (20 g) of salt to dissolve. Add a small scoop of dye from the bath mixed in step 1. To create the *second lightest* color, add two or three more scoops of dye from step 1 into the salted warm water.

For the *second darkest* color, add two or three more scoops of dye from the bath mixed in step 1 into the salted warm water.

Continue adding dye to the bath or diluting with warm water to create even more colors.

Dipping and Tying

You don't have to fully submerge the snapsuit into the dye bath. Try just dipping a section of it for a unique look. Or, prepare several dye baths, and dip different sections into different colors.

Tie-dyeing is much easier than it looks. All you need is a few rubber bands and a little know-how. In the following projects, you'll learn everything from dyeing targets to stripes.

Caring for Dyed Garments

You can machine wash a dyed snapsuit with other clothing without fear of the color bleeding if you follow a few simple steps. Prior to the first wash, run the suit under warm water to be sure all the excess dye is removed, then wash it in cold water with similar-colored items. Remove them from the washer as soon as the load is finished. Hang to dry or tumble dry.

Q & A

Q: *Why do I add salt to the dye?*

A: Salt opens up the pores of the fabric, which allows the dye to be absorbed.

Q: *What is the shelf life of mixed dye?*

A: The shelf life is relatively short and depends on the type of dye you use. Most fiber-reactive dyes have a shelf life of four days once mixed. To store mixed dye, funnel it into a recycled plastic jug, and store it in a refrigerator or cool, dark place.

Q: *What other fabrics dye well?*

A: Besides cotton, linen, silk, nylon, rayon, and wool all dye well. Experiment with different fabrics and dyes for the best results.

Haight and Ashbury

Dyeing stripes is one of the easiest tie-dyeing techniques; all you need is a couple of rubber bands and a dye bath. Combine cool stripes with a hip flocked iron on, and tiny tots will blend right in to the fashion scene in San Francisco.

1. Wet a prepped snapsuit. Working in the center, gather accordion pleats across the chest area. Pinch the area in your hand, and tightly wrap the pinched section with a rubber band or two. Create a second stripe by wrapping a few more rubber bands just below the first one.

2. Following the dye bath instructions on page 11, prepare a turquoise dye bath.

3. Dip the suit into the prepared dye bath, and soak it until it reaches the desired color. Remove from the bath, and remove the rubber bands by cutting them with scissors.

4. Rinse, roll it in an old towel to remove the excess water, and hang to dry.

5. Once dry, add a hippy-style flocked iron-on to the center. For more information on iron-ons, visit chapter 6.

Variation
Little Miss Sunshine

Add stripes to the sleeves by gathering the edge and wrapping it with one or two rubber bands.

Variation
Bold and Blue

Starting with a dyed light gray snapsuit, use eight rubber bands to create a thick stripe in the center and then dip the suit in a deep blue dye bath.

Flower Power

Bright and cheery, this summery design will surely supply a smile...or several. The **double-dip dyeing technique** works well with either coordinating or complementary color combinations.

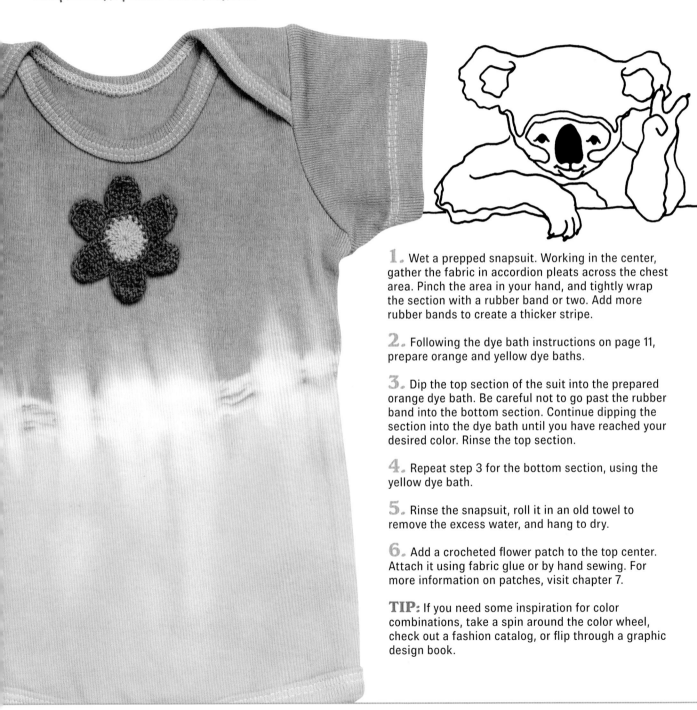

1. Wet a prepped snapsuit. Working in the center, gather the fabric in accordion pleats across the chest area. Pinch the area in your hand, and tightly wrap the section with a rubber band or two. Add more rubber bands to create a thicker stripe.

2. Following the dye bath instructions on page 11, prepare orange and yellow dye baths.

3. Dip the top section of the suit into the prepared orange dye bath. Be careful not to go past the rubber band into the bottom section. Continue dipping the section into the dye bath until you have reached your desired color. Rinse the top section.

4. Repeat step 3 for the bottom section, using the yellow dye bath.

5. Rinse the snapsuit, roll it in an old towel to remove the excess water, and hang to dry.

6. Add a crocheted flower patch to the top center. Attach it using fabric glue or by hand sewing. For more information on patches, visit chapter 7.

TIP: If you need some inspiration for color combinations, take a spin around the color wheel, check out a fashion catalog, or flip through a graphic design book.

Sweet Tweet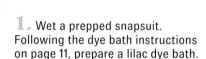

Dipping just the bottom section of a snapsuit into the dye bath—known as **half-dip dyeing**—creates a soft and simple design that keeps the top portion free for a little embellishment, such as an embroidered birdie with a lucky clover.

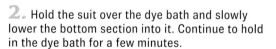

1. Wet a prepped snapsuit. Following the dye bath instructions on page 11, prepare a lilac dye bath.

2. Hold the suit over the dye bath and slowly lower the bottom section into it. Continue to hold in the dye bath for a few minutes.

3. Carefully rinse the bottom of the suit, roll it in an old towel to remove the excess water, and hang to dry.

4. Once dry, use an embroidery hoop and floss (I used pale olive green and dusty pink) to embroider a design. If you want to embroider the bird with a clover, you'll find the template on page 164. Just transfer it to the fabric and go. To embroider an outline, a simple stitch will do, such as the backstitch or split stitch. For more information on embroidery, see page 64.

TIP: If you want a darker color, use a longer dye time. To prevent your hands from getting tired, construct a low clothesline above the dye bath. Use pins to attach the snapsuit to the line, and then adjust the line to the desired height to keep the bottom of the suit in the dye bath.

Bull's Eye

Sweet and swirled, this **target dyeing technique** is easier to recreate than it looks. Instead of dipping into a dye bath, use condiment bottles to squirt dye onto various sections of a gathered snapsuit.

1. Wet a prepped snapsuit. Decide where you want to center your target. Use your fingers to pinch and pull the center of the target into a cone. Tightly wrap a rubber band around the fabric approximately 1 inch (2.5 cm) from the tip of the cone.

2. Continue adding and wrapping rubber bands down to the base of the cone; this creates the stripes of the target.

3. Following the dye bath instructions on page 11, prepare two dye baths, one yellow and one pink. Use a funnel to pour the dyes into separate condiment bottles.

4. Very carefully, squirt one of the bottled dyes onto the tip of the banded cone. Keep applying the dye until you get the color you want. Rinse the area with cold water.

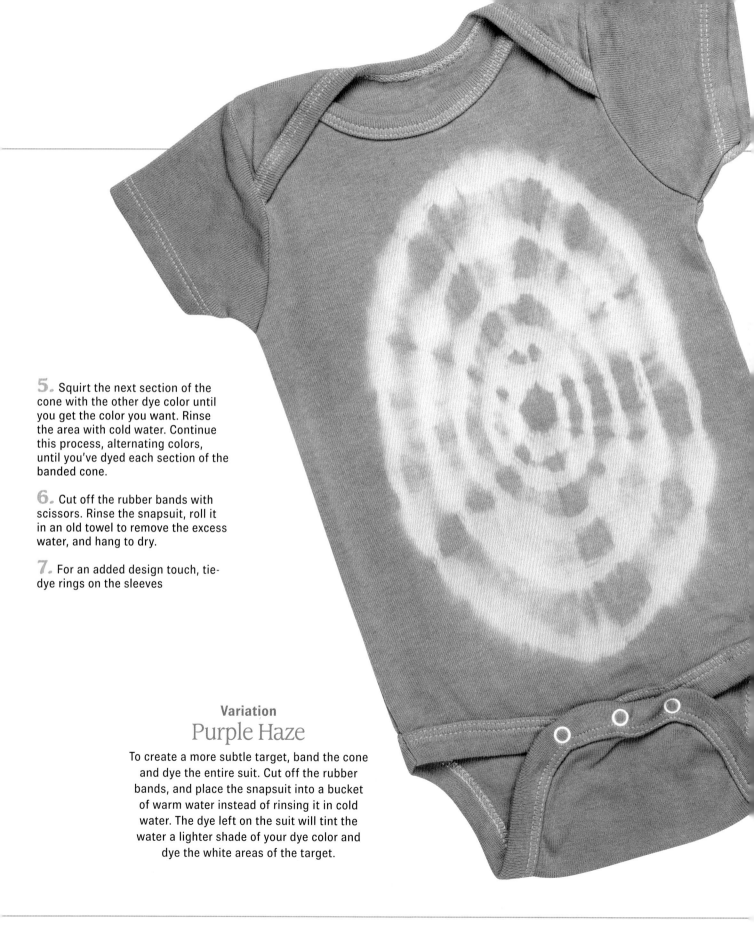

5. Squirt the next section of the cone with the other dye color until you get the color you want. Rinse the area with cold water. Continue this process, alternating colors, until you've dyed each section of the banded cone.

6. Cut off the rubber bands with scissors. Rinse the snapsuit, roll it in an old towel to remove the excess water, and hang to dry.

7. For an added design touch, tie-dye rings on the sleeves

Variation
Purple Haze

To create a more subtle target, band the cone and dye the entire suit. Cut off the rubber bands, and place the snapsuit into a bucket of warm water instead of rinsing it in cold water. The dye left on the suit will tint the water a lighter shade of your dye color and dye the white areas of the target.

Loopy

Circles are one of the first shapes a baby learns. Luckily, they also make a bold design statement. **Dyeing rings** is an easy technique that you can use over and over.

1. Wet a prepped snapsuit. Decide where you want to place the first ring. Use your fingers to pinch and pull the center of the ring to make a cone. Tightly wrap a rubber band around the fabric approximately 1 inch (2.5 cm) from the tip of the cone. For smaller rings, wrap the rubber bands closer to the tip; for larger rings, wrap them farther away.

2. Following the dye bath instructions on page 11, prepare a mauve pink dye bath.

3. Dip the suit into the prepared dye bath, and soak it until you get the color you want.

4. Take the snapsuit out of the bath, rinse it, and cut off the rubber bands with scissors. Rinse again, roll it in an old towel to remove the excess water, and hang to dry.

Variation
Center Star

Frame an embellishment by first dyeing a ring at the top center of a snapsuit. Then place a small patch, iron-on, or an embroidered design in the center of the circle.

With Love from Me to You

I don't know about You, but as a teenager I doodled hearts and love notes all over MY notebooks. Now, with just a few simple folds, You can **tie-dye hearts** onto fabric.

1. Wet a prepped snapsuit. Fold it in half lengthwise, matching sleeve to sleeve.

2. Use a water-soluble fabric marker to draw half of a heart shape on one side of the fold. Accordion fold the fabric along the drawn line, forcing it into a straight line. Tightly wrap one or two rubber bands around the line.

3. Following the dye bath instructions on page 11, prepare a navy dye bath.

4. Dip the suit into the prepared dye bath, and soak it until you get the color you want. Remove it from the bath, rinse it, and remove the rubber bands by cutting them with scissors.

5. Rinse again, roll the suit in an old towel to remove the excess water, and hang to dry.

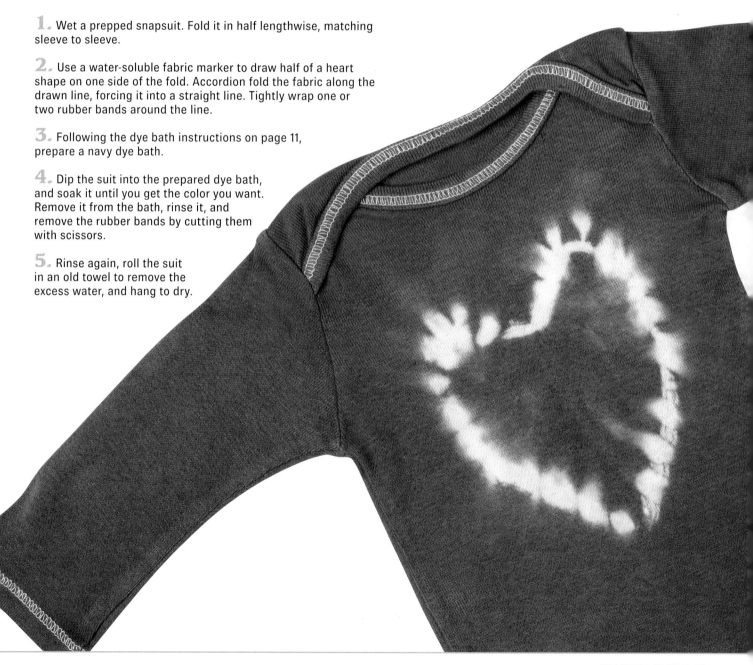

Free Love

Creating a **marbled dye effect** is as simple as scrunching a snapsuit into a ball and wrapping it with rubber bands before dyeing it. You'll get a different look each time.

1. Wet a prepped snapsuit, and separate the front from the back so the fabric is loose. Scrunch the suit into a rough ball. Use approximately 20 rubber bands to shape and wrap the ball in a random pattern.

2. Following the dye bath instructions on page 11, prepare a purple dye bath. Soak the snapsuit in the prepared dye bath until the desired color is reached.

3. Remove from the bath, rinse, and remove the rubber bands by cutting them with scissors. Rinse the snapsuit again, roll it in an old towel to remove excess water, and hang to dry.

4. Once dry, attach an iron-on winged-heart patch following the manufacturer's instructions. For more information about iron-ons, visit chapter 6.

Variation
Santa Barbara

Inspired by the colors of grapes hanging on the vines in Santa Barbara, this snapsuit features spring green and burgundy red. First dye the suit in green, then marble it in burgundy.

Night Fall

Instead of messy hot wax, use a bottled resist formula to create a **simple batik** design. You can find it at craft shops wherever dye is sold. From my experience, I've found this resist works best when making basic, bold shapes.

1. Place a layer of tin foil inside a dry prepped snapsuit to prevent bleed through. Apply the resist formula to the fabric to make the star and dot pattern. You can apply it directly to the fabric by squeezing the bottle, or you can use a paintbrush. Let it dry completely.

2. Following the dye bath instructions on page 11, prepare a baby blue dye bath. Wet the suit before placing it in the dye bath to soak until the desired color is reached.

3. Rinse and wash with warm soapy water until the resist washes off. To care for the snapsuit, wash as normal.

4. Once dry, use an embroidery needle and floss to add a running stitch (page 64) around the neck for a little extra pop.

Whale of a Good Time

This technique, known as **un-dyeing**, lets you draw designs directly on dyed fabric using a bleach pen. You can draw freehand or use a stencil.

1. Following the dye bath instructions on page 11, prepare a salmon dye bath.

2. Wet a prepped snapsuit and soak it in the salmon dye bath until the desired color is reached. Rinse the suit, roll it in an old towel to remove the excess water, and hang to dry.

3. Once dry, place a piece of tin foil inside the snapsuit to prevent the bleach from seeping through to the other side.

4. With the skinny tip of a bleach pen, draw swirls and polka dots on the top center section. Wait approximately three to five minutes before rinsing quickly in cold water.

5. Once dry, apply a felt whale appliqué by hand sewing. You'll find the template for the appliqué on page 164. Use gem glue to attach a rhinestone for the eye. For more information on felt appliqués, visit chapter 3.

TIP: If you want a more graphic design than one made by drawing freehand, make your own stencil using shelf-liner paper. For more information on stencils, see page 28.

Honey Bear

Dyeing to match? Color your snapsuit to match the iron-on or appliqué elements you plan to use. This technique is a great way to create design cohesion.

1. Following the dye bath instructions on page 11, prepare gold and brown dye baths.

TIP: To get your dye bath where you want it, first dissolve the dye full-strength in a paper cup. Then slowly add the dissolved dye to a bucket of hot water, testing the color with paper towels as you go, until you get the color you want.

2. Wet a prepped snapsuit. Dye it in the gold dye bath until the desired color is reached. Rinse and remove any excess water by rolling it in an old towel.

3. Use rubber bands to add random patterned stripes. For more information on dyeing stripes, see page 14.

4. Dip the suit into the brown dye bath and soak until the desired color is reached. Remove from the bath, rinse, and cut off the rubber bands.

5. Rinse, roll the suit in an old towel to remove excess water, and hang to dry.

6. Once dry, appliqué a cutout—this one was recycled from an old T-shirt—to the snapsuit by either hand or machine sewing. For more information on appliqués, visit chapter 3.

B A S I C S

Chapter 2
Painting

Painting is a great way to turn a snapsuit into an original work of art. But you don't have to be a van Gogh to paint these fabulous fabric designs.

Types of Paint

Fabric paint is available in a variety of textures, styles, and forms, including paint pens and markers, dimensional paint, and brush-on paint. You can find it at most craft and fabric stores in every color imaginable. No matter what type you select, be sure to choose paint that is nontoxic and machine washable. All fabric paint must be heat set in order to be washable. When heat setting, follow the manufacturer's instructions for the particular paint you're using. For mixed application snapsuits that combine paint and patches or iron-ons, you may also need to use a pressing cloth.

Brush-On Fabric Paint

Brush-on fabric paint is applied directly to the garment with a paintbrush, foam paintbrush, sponge, or stamp. When dried, brush-on paint generally remains soft and flexible on the garment. Available in matte, pearl, glitter, or shiny finishes, this type of paint works well with stencils, foam stamps, and free-form painting.

If you can't find the color you want, simply make your own by blending acrylic paint with a fabric paint medium, found in art and craft stores in the artists paint section. Follow the rules of the color wheel to blend paint colors to create new shades, or add a drop or two of white to lighten the colors.

Dimensional Fabric Paint

This paint is perfect for lettering, outlining, and adding dimension to a brush-on painted design, and it typically comes in a squeeze bottle with a fine tip.

Dimensional fabric paint appears thicker than the brush-on paint; it is also available in a variety of finishes including shiny, glitter, pearl, matte, and even puffy.

When working with dimensional paints, *never* shake the bottle. This will create air bubbles that could explode onto your design. If the tip of the bottle gets clogged, poke it with a long sewing pin or paperclip. I always like to start my bottle on a scrap piece of paper before beginning on the fabric. If you notice an air bubble in your painted design, pop it with a sewing pin while the paint is still wet. Be sure to heat set the paint, and launder the painted snapsuit inside out.

Paint Pens and Fabric Markers

For lettering or fine details, I like to use fabric paint pens and markers. They are just like regular markers, only the ink and paint are designed for fabric. You can get these pens in a variety of colors and glitters. Always heat set the ink from the pens and markers before you wash the suit.

Fabric Paintbrushes

When painting on fabric, use a brush that is specifically designed for working with fabric. These brushes are stiffer, allowing you to press the paint into the fabric so it clings to the fibers.

For stenciling, pick a stencil brush. This brush has short, firmly packed bristles, which reduce the chances of getting paint under the edge of the stencil because of the stiff bristles.

Wooden-handled foam paintbrushes are great for applying paint to foam stamps, fruits, and vegetables or for stenciling. They are inexpensive and can be bought in bulk at most craft stores.

Painting Techniques

Be bold! There are no rules for painting. Don't worry about perfection: sometimes mistakes lead to happy endings. Try using techniques in combination to expand your design potential. For each of these techniques, make sure you insert a piece of waxed paper between the front and back of the snapsuit prior to painting. This prevents the paint from seeping through to the other side.

Stencil Painting

Working with stencils is a quick and easy way to paint a snapsuit. Stencils are available in letters, words, shapes, and all-over designs. You'll find an array of baby-themed stencils at fabric and craft stores.

When choosing a stencil, think about the size and placement. The front or back of the suit is a great place for a large stencil while the upper shoulder or sleeve areas need a smaller stencil. Once you've chosen your stencil placement, secure it to the fabric by either pressing and holding while you paint, adding a piece of low-tack masking tape to the edges of the stencil, or by applying repositionable stencil adhesive to the back of the stencil.

Lining up individual letter stencils can be tricky. I like to begin by drawing a line on the suit using a water-soluble fabric marker with disappearing ink and a clear ruler. Center all the letters on the line, and then secure each stencil with low-tack tape.

Once your stencil is secured to the fabric, you're ready to paint. Remember to place a layer of waxed paper between the front and back of the garment. The key to good stencil painting is not using very much paint. It is better to do two light coats than one heavy coat. I like to squirt a little paint on a palette, dab the brush into the paint, and tap off any excess paint until the brush is dry. If you overload your brush, the paint might seep under the stencil, creating a sloppy and uneven edge. For best results, paint over the stencil in an up-and-down fashion, never side to side.

If the stencil designs on the market are not what you're looking for, you can easily create your own stencil with self-adhesive shelf liner. The wing pattern on Angel Baby (page 32) was achieved with a black and white copy and some clear shelf liner.

Freehand Painting

Don't be discouraged by the idea of painting freehand. You don't need to be a professional painter to get outstanding results. I like to work with paint pens and markers for this technique because it feels just like doodling on paper. For brushed-on designs, be sure to use fabric paintbrushes when painting freehand so the paint will properly adhere to the snapsuit. If you need design ideas, look at clip art, greeting cards, and scrapbook papers.

Stamping

You can stamp your fabric with anything from traditional foam stamps and household items to fruits and vegetables. Foam stamps are available at craft and fabric shops and come in a variety of shapes and styles. You can find large letter stamps like the one used on T Is For Tommy (page 41) or stamps with all-over designs like the one used on Ahoy Mate (page 40). Foam stamps are often very inexpensive; plus, they can be cleaned with soap and water and used over and over again.

When painting with foam stamps, pour some fabric paint onto a plastic plate and dip the foam stamp into it (or brush paint directly onto the foam). Then press the stamp onto the fabric and gently lift the stamp to reveal the painted design. Allow the paint to dry, and heat set it according to the manufacturer's instructions. You can layer different paint colors on the same stamp for a more colorful design.

I really enjoy stamping and painting with found objects and everyday items. Pencils and hot glue sticks create perfect polka dots, spaghetti creates fine lines, and keys look very cutting edge. When you pull the item off the fabric, revealing the design below, you never know what you'll get. It's always best to experiment; try testing the stamp on a paper towel or a scrap of fabric first.

One of my first art projects as a child was stamping with potatoes, and I still find myself stamping with vegetables to this day. There is something organic and simple about the impression made by fruits and veggies. Potatoes and carrots can be carved to create shapes, ends of celery create beautiful flower shapes, and apples create wonderful impressions. You can see the results on Crab Apple, May Flowers, and Rose Parade on pages 36 and 37.

When painting with fruits, vegetables, or household items, apply the paint directly to the item with a foam paintbrush instead of dipping the item in the paint; this creates a cleaner stamped impression. Once the paint is applied to the stamp, press the stamp onto the snapsuit and gently lift it off again. Allow the paint to dry, and heat set it according to the manufacturer's instructions.

Q & A

Q: *Can I mix different brands of fabric paints?*

A: Absolutely! I have mixed various brands of fabric paint with great results. If you're not sure about a certain paint, just test it first on a scrap of fabric.

Q: *Why is prewashing so important before painting?*

A: You must prewash to remove the sizing from the snapsuit. Sizing is a combination of starches and stiffeners applied to a garment or bolt of fabric so it will look better at the retail store. Sizing must be removed or it will interfere with the fabric's ability to absorb the paint.

11 Carnival Nights

Love is even better under the big top! For this design, you'll use **store-bought stencils** to paint letters over a simple tie-dyed snapsuit.

1. Tie-dye a white snapsuit with black dye using the marbled technique on page 22. When it's dry, align the stencil in your desired position. Use small pieces of low-tack tape to secure it.

2. Dab a stencil brush in hot pink brush-on fabric paint. Tap off any excess. Working up and down, tap the brush over the stencil. Don't brush the paint side to side.

3. Allow the paint to dry, remove the stencil, and follow the manufacturer's instructions to heat set the paint.

Variation
Garden Finds

Layer metallic paints as you stencil. For the caterpillar, I began with a coat of medium green paint. I then layered metallic gold and blue paint over the green to add highlights. I used two drops of dimensional paint for eyes.

Punky

When you want a slightly edgier look, **reverse-stencil painting** is the way to go. It allows the letters to remain legible while giving you a nice feathered edge. Look for sticky-back foam letters, or purchase large sheets of foam to make your own font.

1. Leaving room for the iron-on, use a ruler to align the foam letters before sticking them to the snapsuit.

2. Dab a stencil brush in white brush-on fabric paint. Tap off the excess. Working up and down, tap the brush over and around the foam letters. When you get to the edges, feather the paint using short brush strokes.

3. Add details to the neckline by lightly brushing the paint along the ribbing.

4. Allow the paint to dry and remove the foam letters. Follow the manufacturer's instructions to heat set the paint.

5. Add a skull iron-on to complete the design. For more information about iron-ons, visit chapter 6.

Angel Baby

Make your own stencils using clear self-stick shelf liner. For ease of cutting, always use a sharp craft knife and a self-healing mat. And for other design ideas, look to clip art or coloring books.

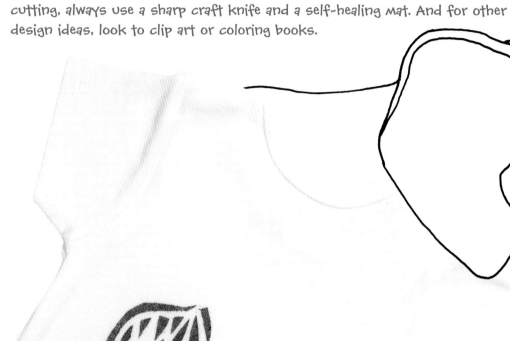

1. Copy the template on page 165. Lay the shelf liner over the template and tape them together. Tape both pieces to the self-healing mat. Use the sharp craft knife to cut out the design.

2. Using a ruler as a guide, align and stick the cutout design to the *back* of the snapsuit.

3. Dab a stencil brush in metallic plum fabric paint. You want to work with a semi-dry brush, so tap off the excess paint. Working up and down, tap the brush over the stencil.

4. Allow the paint to dry. Peel off the stencil liner and follow the manufacturer's instructions to heat set the paint.

I Love the 80s

Want to paint like Jackson Pollock? Then **splatter painting** is the technique to try. It's so easy, and the results are different every time.

1. Working outside, place the snapsuit on an opened plastic garbage bag.

2. For each color of brush-on fabric paint (I used bright yellow, dark turquoise, and red), put two to three large squirts of paint into a small zip-top plastic bag. Add 3 teaspoons (15 mL) of water to the bag. Seal the baggie, and then squeeze it to blend the water and paint together.

3. Stand over the suit to work. Snip the corner off one of the baggies, and splatter the paint in a random pattern. Do the same with the other two colors.

4. Allow the paint to dry. Follow the manufacturer's instructions to heat set the paints.

TIP: This is a great technique to try with a toddler who wants to help design. Just make sure he or she is wearing painting clothes!

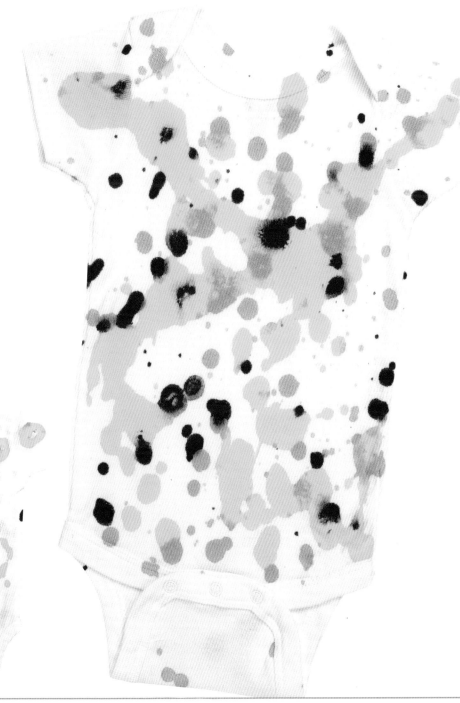

  # Princess

In my house, nothing is off limits when it comes to crafting. For the following projects, I **stamped with household objects** such as hot glue sticks, pencils, paper cups, and keys to create the designs.

1. Using a foam paintbrush, apply purple brush-on fabric paint to a foam crown stamp. Stamp it on the snapsuit in a diamond pattern or pattern of your choice. Apply more paint to the stamp as needed. Allow the paint to dry. Add highlights to the stamped crowns using gold glitter dimensional fabric paint.

2. Pour a pool of metallic gold brush-on fabric paint onto a paper plate. Dip the eraser end of a pencil into the paint. Stamp the eraser on the suit. Continue until you have filled in the design area as desired.

3. Allow the paints to dry. Follow the manufacturer's instructions to heat set the paint.

Variation
Key to My Heart

To create a little rocker necklace, apply paint to a key, then stamp it on the top center of the snapsuit. Add the beads by dipping the end of the glue stick into brush-on fabric paint and stamping dots on either side of the key.

Variation
Ring Around

Get perfect circles every time by using paper or plastic cups to create rings. Pour a little paint onto a paper plate, dip the edge of a cup into the paint, and stamp on the fabric. Other items that stamp well are buttons, washers, kitchen utensils, leaves, and coins.

 # Crab Apple

As a child, **stamping with fruits and veggies** was one of my first experiences with art. Now I love using them because of the simple and natural designs they make.

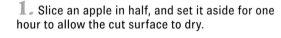

1. Slice an apple in half, and set it aside for one hour to allow the cut surface to dry.

2. Using a foam paintbrush, apply a thick coat of red brush-on fabric paint to the apple. Stamp the apple on the *back* of the snapsuit near the top.

3. Use a dark brown fabric marker to draw the stem and seeds. Use a tan fabric marker to draw a line under the stem to add depth.

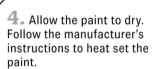

4. Allow the paint to dry. Follow the manufacturer's instructions to heat set the paint.

5. Apply iron-on letters underneath the stamped apple to spell CRAB.

Variation
May Flowers

Using a paring knife, carve hearts, letters, stars, or flowers into carrots. For this design, carve four V-shaped notches into the edges of the carrot to make the flower shape. Use a different color paint for each flower.

Variation
Rose Parade

The stamp for the large rose was made from the bottom of a bunch of celery. Cut the celery approximately 3 inches (7.6 cm) from the bottom, and allow it to dry for an hour prior to stamping. Add some curlicues using green dimensional fabric paint.

  # Buddha-ful

When you use low-tack tape as your guideline, **lettering with fabric paint pens** is as easy as writing on paper. Pair some clever wording with a simple iron-on, and you've got yourself a beauty!

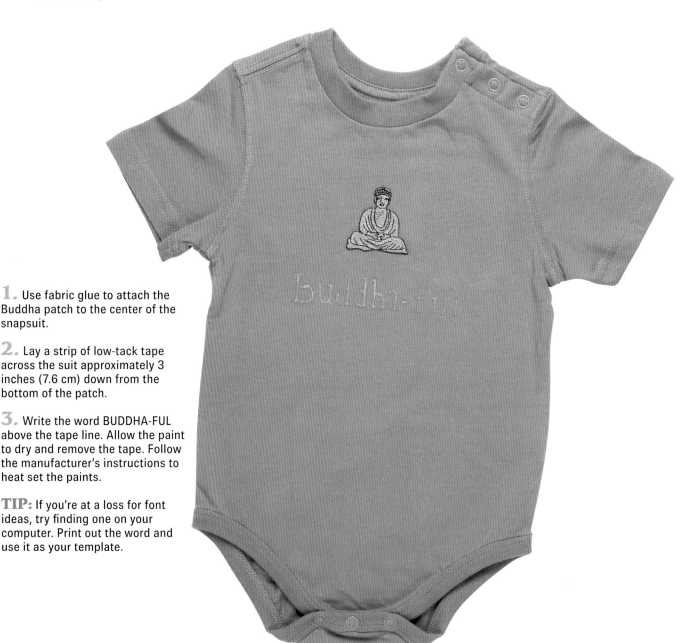

1. Use fabric glue to attach the Buddha patch to the center of the snapsuit.

2. Lay a strip of low-tack tape across the suit approximately 3 inches (7.6 cm) down from the bottom of the patch.

3. Write the word BUDDHA-FUL above the tape line. Allow the paint to dry and remove the tape. Follow the manufacturer's instructions to heat set the paints.

TIP: If you're at a loss for font ideas, try finding one on your computer. Print out the word and use it as your template.

Cherry Blossom

Soft and sweet, this design is so easy you won't even need a paintbrush. Create the branches by doing some **freehand drawing with fabric markers** directly on the snapsuit. Then make the blossoms from dots of paint applied using your fingertips.

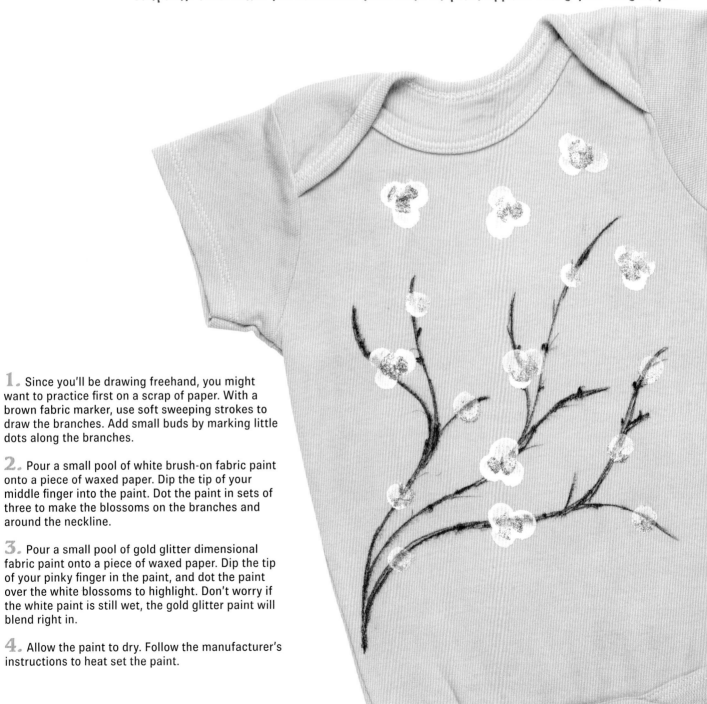

1. Since you'll be drawing freehand, you might want to practice first on a scrap of paper. With a brown fabric marker, use soft sweeping strokes to draw the branches. Add small buds by marking little dots along the branches.

2. Pour a small pool of white brush-on fabric paint onto a piece of waxed paper. Dip the tip of your middle finger into the paint. Dot the paint in sets of three to make the blossoms on the branches and around the neckline.

3. Pour a small pool of gold glitter dimensional fabric paint onto a piece of waxed paper. Dip the tip of your pinky finger in the paint, and dot the paint over the white blossoms to highlight. Don't worry if the white paint is still wet, the gold glitter paint will blend right in.

4. Allow the paint to dry. Follow the manufacturer's instructions to heat set the paint.

# Ahoy Mate

You can purchase **themed foam stamps** in many different shapes and styles. I fell in love with the pirate-themed stamps—the ship and skull and crossbones—and knew they would look great on a darker snapsuit.

1. Apply brush-on fabric paints to different parts of the ship stamp. For this design I used black for the base and pole of the ship, white for the sails, and dark tan for the flag. Press the stamp onto the fabric.

2. Apply red brush-on fabric paint to the skull stamp. Press the stamp onto the snapsuit in a random pattern around the ship.

3. Use a green fabric marker to draw broken lines from the ship to the skulls. Add a light brushing of dark orange brush-on fabric paint to the sails to add depth. Use dimensional fabric paint and silver glitter brush-on fabric paint to add highlights to the ship and sails.

4. Allow the paint to dry. Follow the manufacturer's instructions to heat set the paint.

Variation
T Is for Tommy

Small foam stamps are perfect for painting on sleeves or for creating an allover design, but also try oversized wall stamps like the big "T" in this design. I layered yellow and blue brush-on fabric paint to make soft green shades and highlights.

Variation
Black Sheep

When I saw the sheep stamp, the first thing I thought of was black sheep. I used black brush-on fabric paint for the stamp and added a little turquoise paint for the eye.

20 Off to the Moon

Using **dimensional fabric paint** can add highlights and depth to your design. Outline a shape, or blend the paints together with a toothpick to create a marbled effect.

1. Use a purchased rocket ship stamp. With a foam paintbrush, apply red, blue, and yellow brush-on fabric paint to the stamp. Press the stamp onto the fabric at the desired position. Allow to dry.

2. Using dimensional fabric paint in coordinating colors, highlight the edges of the rocket ship. Paint silver lines with dimensional paint at the edge of the ship.

3. Outline the flames with yellow dimensional fabric paint. Fill in the outline with a thicker coat of orange dimensional paint. Use a toothpick to blend the two colors.

4. Draw a few yellow stars by hand around the rocket ship. Allow all the paints to dry. Follow the manufacturer's instructions to heat set the paints.

TIP: When combining dimensional paints for a marbled effect, use shiny and pearlized paints for extra sheen and luster.

Variation
Z Is for Zebra

Dimensional paint in squeeze bottles makes lettering a snap. For this design I wrote Zs around a sewn-on zebra patch that I found in the baby section at the fabric store. I thought the brown and orange in the patch would look great on a dyed yellow snapsuit.

Chapter 3

Appliqué

Appliqué is one of my favorite ways to alter snapsuits. It's an easy decorative technique that entails attaching one fabric to another. The wide variety of printed and patterned fabrics makes creating appliqués fun, and, since you only need a small piece, it's also easy on the wallet. There are all sorts of advanced appliqué techniques, but I'm focusing on quick and easy ideas—including hand and machine sewing as well as painting— that can be completed in minutes with outstanding results.

A Sticky Situation

I like to use lightweight paper-backed fusible webbing for making my appliqués. Much like double-sided tape, it has two adhesive surfaces, making it the perfect material for creating and applying appliqués with ease. Heat from your iron melts the adhesive, which allows it to stick to the fabric. You simply fuse the fabric for the appliqué to one side of the webbing, cut out a design, remove the paper backing, and fuse it to the snapsuit.

Prewash the appliqué fabric and the suit prior to applying the fusible webbing. Make sure you read the manufacturer's instructions for use. Once you've fused your fabric, you'll need to finish the edge with a hand stitch, machine stitch, or dimensional fabric paint.

Machine-Stitched Appliqué

Use basic polyester or cotton thread for this technique, or mix it up and use silk, shiny, or variegated threads to create a unique edge. Because the snapsuits are made from a knit fabric, use a ballpoint needle to avoid creating snags or holes while you sew.

The three basic stitches for machine appliqué are the straight stitch, zigzag, and satin stitch. No matter which stitch you use, the process is the same—just stitch around the edge of the appliqué until it's secured to the fabric.

Straight Stitch

When using a straight stitch to sew your appliqué, you can either turn the edge of the appliqué under prior to stitching for a finished look, or you can leave the edges raw and let them fray with laundering for a more artsy look.

Zigzag Stitch

This stitch adds a more textured look to a project. You can set your stitch to various widths for different looks.

Satin Stitch

When you want a beautiful, polished edge, use the satin stitch, which is basically a shortened zigzag stitch. To make it, set the length of your zigzag stitch to the lowest, or almost lowest, setting. The width of the stitch can vary, depending on the look you want. Make sure the stitch is wide enough to catch the edge of the snapsuit fabric and at least 1/16 inch (1.6 mm) into the appliqué.

Hand-Stitched Appliqué

Hand-stitched appliqué is a quick way to add pop. I like to use embroidery floss and a ballpoint needle. When working with embroidery floss, I separate the threads and only work with two or three strands at a time, depending on the line thickness I want. The easiest stitches for hand appliqué are the running stitch and the whipstitch. Look for them in the stitch guide on page 65.

Dimensional Fabric Paint Appliqué

Using dimensional fabric paint is a quick and easy way to seal the edges of the appliqué. The paints are available in tons of colors and textures. For a unique look, use shiny or glitter dimensional fabric paint— just be sure all your paints are non-toxic!

Q&A

Q: *What's better, hand or machine appliqué?*

A: Both techniques are equally good looking and easy. It really depends on the look you want. For a more homespun or funky look, I like to hand stitch. Machine stitching is a little more polished and looks great on dressy snapsuits. I also like to combine the techniques. You can see what that looks like on My Daddy Rocks (page 130).

Q: *What are the care considerations for appliquéd suits?*

A: If you've prewashed the appliqué fabric, you can launder normally. When ironing, you'll probably need to use a pressing cloth on the appliqués if they're shiny, metallic, satin, or heat-transferred. Printed, dyed, and silk-screened fabrics should be okay without one. Always test a corner of the appliqué first. If the iron sticks, lower the heat setting, and bring out the cloth.

  # Marrakesh

By combining a **machine-stitched appliqué** with glitter paint and flocked iron-ons, you can create a boutique-style snapsuit. Use satin thread in your sewing machine to add extra shine to the satin stitch.

1. Cut out a motif from a Moroccan-inspired cotton fabric. Leave at least a 1-inch (2.5 cm) allowance around the edges.

2. Cut a piece of lightweight paper-backed fusible web to fit the cutout. Follow the manufacturer's instructions to fuse the webbing to the wrong side of the fabric.

3. Cut out the motif by cutting away the allowance you left in step 1. Remove the paper backing, and place the appliqué in the desired position. Follow the manufacturer's instructions to fuse the appliqué to the fabric. If needed, use a pressing cloth over the motif.

4. Position bird iron-ons slightly over the edge of your fabric design. Adhere them following the manufacturer's instructions. For more information on iron-ons, visit chapter 6.

5. Thread your machine with satin thread and use the satin stitch (page 45) to sew around the edges. Do not sew over the bird iron-ons.

6. Use a paintbrush to apply gold glitter fabric paint to the motif to highlight the fabric. Dry flat overnight. For more information on glitter paint, visit Chapter 2.

Variation

Doodled Love

Stitch it funky! Instead of using a satin stitch, use a long, wide zigzag stitch for a relaxed look.

 Play Ball

Football is big in my house, so this **hand-stitched appliqué** helmet seemed like a natural choice. Show your spirit by making it in your team colors. If football isn't your game, swap the helmet for a soccer ball.

1. Copy the templates on page 165 and cut them out. Cut an 8-inch (20.3 cm) square from 100 percent cotton fabric. Cut a 7-inch (17.8 cm) square of lightweight paper-backed fusible web. Follow the manufacturer's instructions to fuse the webbing to the wrong side of the fabric.

2. Using the background template as your guide, trace it in reverse on the paper backing of the fusible web, and cut it out. Remove the paper backing and place the appliqué on the fabric in the desired position. Adhere to the snapsuit following the manufacturer's instructions.

3. Thread an embroidery needle with two strands of embroidery floss. Sew around the outer edge of the background appliqué using a running stitch (page 64).

4. Trace the helmet template onto a piece of felt, and cut it out. Attach the helmet to the center of the background appliqué using fabric glue. Allow the glue to dry.

5. Apply iron-on sport uniform numbers to the back following the manufacturer's instructions. For more information on iron-ons, visit chapter 6.

I Scream

Give your snapsuit soft, pillowy dimension with **puffy appliqué**. This technique works best for simple shapes like circles, squares, and triangles.

1. Cut a triangle for the cone from a scrap of brown knit fabric. Sew the cone to the front by hand using brown embroidery floss and the running stitch (page 65).

2. Use a glass to trace two circles on pink knit fabric, then cut them out. Place the two circles with right sides facing. Use a needle and pink thread to hand sew the two circles together. Work as close to the edge as possible, and leave a small opening for turning.

3. Turn the sewn circles right side out, and lightly stuff the shape with polyester fiberfill. Stitch the opening closed.

4. Position the circle on top of the cone, and hand sew it to the snapsuit. Embellish the design with hand-sewn rickrack.

5. Above the ice cream, follow the manufacturer's instructions to attach iron-on letters that spell I SCREAM. For more information on iron-ons, visit chapter 6.

Tattoo Love

Re-crafting old T-shirts is a great way to recycle and make something new. Look for old shirts with motifs that will fit on a snapsuit. Use a variety of machine or hand stitches to add detail to the design.

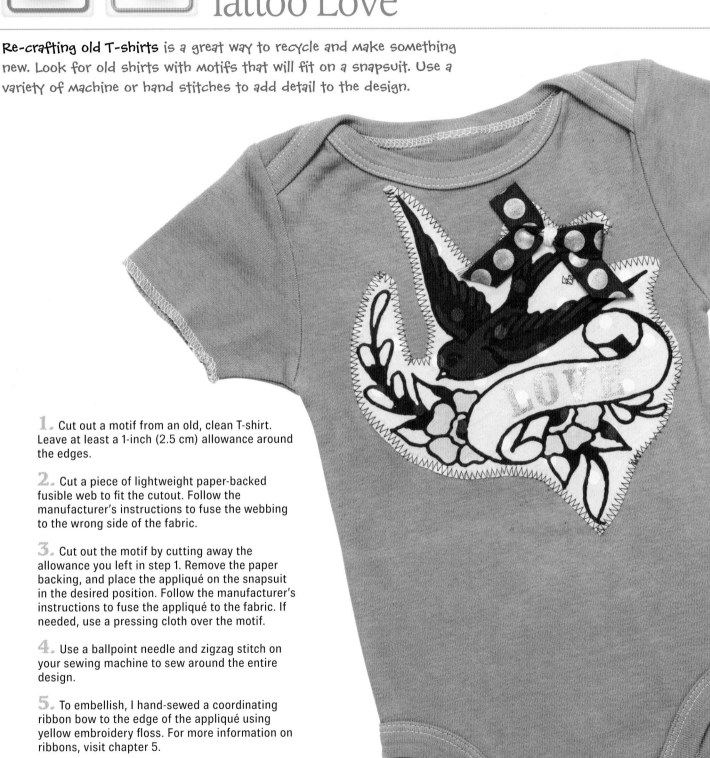

1. Cut out a motif from an old, clean T-shirt. Leave at least a 1-inch (2.5 cm) allowance around the edges.

2. Cut a piece of lightweight paper-backed fusible web to fit the cutout. Follow the manufacturer's instructions to fuse the webbing to the wrong side of the fabric.

3. Cut out the motif by cutting away the allowance you left in step 1. Remove the paper backing, and place the appliqué on the snapsuit in the desired position. Follow the manufacturer's instructions to fuse the appliqué to the fabric. If needed, use a pressing cloth over the motif.

4. Use a ballpoint needle and zigzag stitch on your sewing machine to sew around the entire design.

5. To embellish, I hand-sewed a coordinating ribbon bow to the edge of the appliqué using yellow embroidery floss. For more information on ribbons, visit chapter 5.

Variation
Guitar Star

Try layering motifs for more interest. This design was made basically the same way as Tattoo Love. I layered the guitar motif over the wing shape and used a straight stitch around the edges instead of a zigzag.

Variation
Green Is Good

I used a simple hand stitch with embroidery floss to secure the design to the snapsuit. The raw edge of the knit motif will curl slightly after washing for a soft edge.

Slow Down

Felt appliqués are super cute and super easy. Felt edges don't ravel, it's available in every color imaginable, and it's easy to sew. You can buy it off the bolt, but precut squares may be the just the size you need.

1. Copy the template on page 166 and cut it out. Use the template as a guide to cut the body of the turtle from olive green felt and the remaining pieces from hot pink felt.

2. Position the cutouts on the center front of the snapsuit. Attach them with lime green and hot pink embroidery floss using the running stitch (page 64).

3. Cut a small heart from cream felt. Stitch the heart to the turtle with plum embroidery floss.

Variation
Yee Haw

Look for faux tooled-leather felt to make a Western-style suit. Cut the felt yoke, and stitch it to the front or back. Hand sew an appliqué of boots and spurs beneath the yoke and off to the side.

This **3-D appliqué technique** is seriously "outside the stitch" when it comes to traditional appliqué. Use it as inspiration to create other unique looks.

1. Copy the patterns for the tie on page 166 and cut them out. Use them to cut two pieces each from a printed alphabet fabric.

2. Place the two knots with right sides facing. Sew the edges along the wide top and the two sides, leaving the narrow bottom open. Clip the corners and turn right side out. Press if needed.

3. Place the two tie pieces right sides facing, and sew around all edges, leaving a small opening for turning. Clip the corners and turn right side out. Hand sew the opening closed.

4. Pinch the knot at its bottom to make a small pleat. Wrap the top of the tie around it, and hand sew in place.

5. Center the tie on the snapsuit. Working on just the bottom layer of the tie, hand sew it to the fabric. Use small stitches to sew all the way around the edges.

TIP: If you need a dressy outfit for a wedding or special party, alter this design by making the tie in black satin or in a color that coordinates with the event.

  # Lux Luv

Create kiddy-couture **appliqués with printed fabrics**. Look for interesting motifs—anything from funky chandeliers to sock monkeys—and simply cut them out. You don't need much fabric, so search the remnant bins first.

1. Cut out a motif from a printed fabric. Leave at least a 1-inch (2.5 cm) allowance around the edges.

2. Cut a piece of lightweight paper-backed fusible web to fit the cutout. Follow the manufacturer's instructions to fuse the webbing to the wrong side of the fabric.

3. Cut out the motif by cutting away the allowance you left in step 1. Remove the paper backing and place the appliqué on the snapsuit in the desired position. Follow the manufacturer's instructions to fuse the appliqué to the fabric. If needed, use a pressing cloth over the motif.

4. Machine sew around the edges of the appliqué using a straight, zigzag, or satin stitch (page 46).

5. Follow the manufacturer's instructions to attach metallic iron-on letters that spell XO and LUV. For more information on iron-ons, visit chapter 6.

Variation
The Great

Dye the snapsuit to match a color in your appliqué. I dyed this one to match Beethoven's collar. I turned the edges of the appliqué under and hand sewed it to the fabric.

Beethoven

# Mars Awaits

If you're stuck coming up with a good idea for an appliqué, try using **themed print fabrics as shape inspiration**. When I saw this alien print, I naturally thought of a rocket ship.

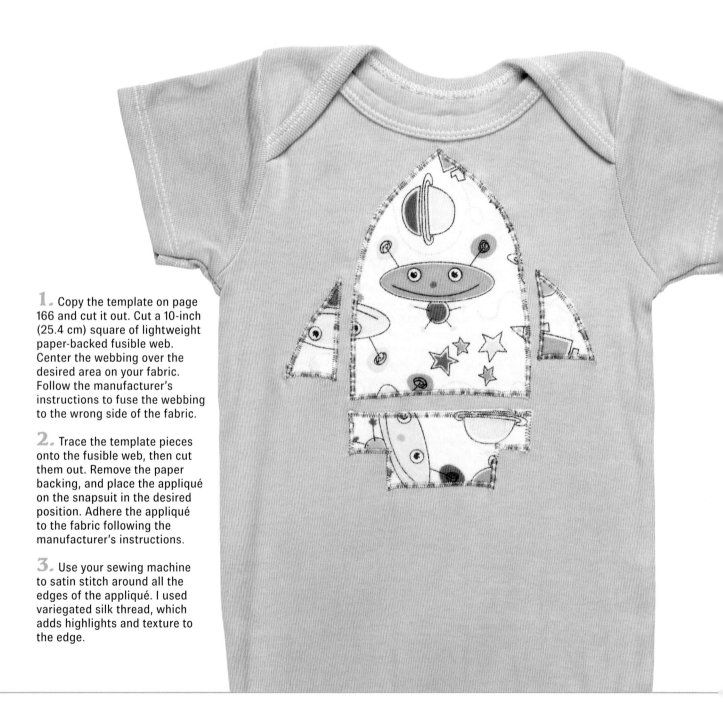

1. Copy the template on page 166 and cut it out. Cut a 10-inch (25.4 cm) square of lightweight paper-backed fusible web. Center the webbing over the desired area on your fabric. Follow the manufacturer's instructions to fuse the webbing to the wrong side of the fabric.

2. Trace the template pieces onto the fusible web, then cut them out. Remove the paper backing, and place the appliqué on the snapsuit in the desired position. Adhere the appliqué to the fabric following the manufacturer's instructions.

3. Use your sewing machine to satin stitch around all the edges of the appliqué. I used variegated silk thread, which adds highlights and texture to the edge.

Like a shortcut? Who doesn't! **Finishing appliqué edges with dimensional fabric paint** offers a quick no-sew alternative to stitching.

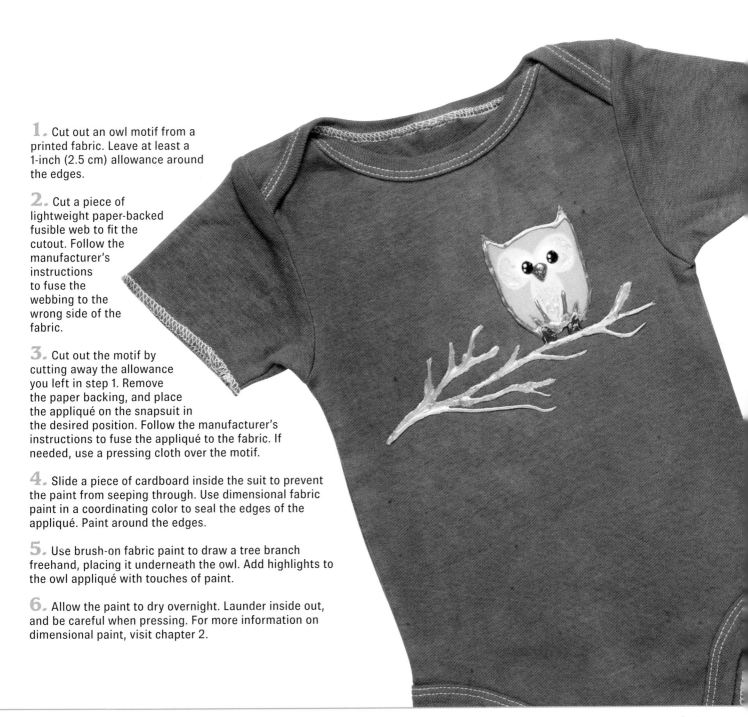

1. Cut out an owl motif from a printed fabric. Leave at least a 1-inch (2.5 cm) allowance around the edges.

2. Cut a piece of lightweight paper-backed fusible web to fit the cutout. Follow the manufacturer's instructions to fuse the webbing to the wrong side of the fabric.

3. Cut out the motif by cutting away the allowance you left in step 1. Remove the paper backing, and place the appliqué on the snapsuit in the desired position. Follow the manufacturer's instructions to fuse the appliqué to the fabric. If needed, use a pressing cloth over the motif.

4. Slide a piece of cardboard inside the suit to prevent the paint from seeping through. Use dimensional fabric paint in a coordinating color to seal the edges of the appliqué. Paint around the edges.

5. Use brush-on fabric paint to draw a tree branch freehand, placing it underneath the owl. Add highlights to the owl appliqué with touches of paint.

6. Allow the paint to dry overnight. Launder inside out, and be careful when pressing. For more information on dimensional paint, visit chapter 2.

Loco Motion

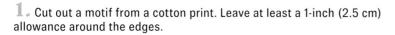
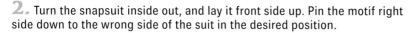

Reverse appliqué draws the eye into the design's details. With washings, the cut, raw edges of the knit material roll for a deconstructed look. This is also great technique for working around a large stain.

1. Cut out a motif from a cotton print. Leave at least a 1-inch (2.5 cm) allowance around the edges.

2. Turn the snapsuit inside out, and lay it front side up. Pin the motif right side down to the wrong side of the suit in the desired position.

3. Sew through both layers following the edge of the appliqué.

4. Turn the snapsuit right side out. Approximately ½ inch (1.3 cm) in from the stitching line, cut away the knit fabric to reveal the appliqué underneath.

5. Add an extra detail by hand sewing a patch to the appliqué.

Variation

Kokeshi

Here I repeated a simple design element for more visual impact using reverse appliqué and some super cute print fabric.

Chapter 4
Embroidery

Embroidery is the art of adorning and decorating clothing, fabrics, and home goods with yarn, thread, and embroidery floss. But you don't need years of experience to get outstanding results. All you need is to learn a few basic stitches. With a little practice, you'll be well on your way to making your own embroidered snapsuits.

Embroidery Tools and Materials

You'll only need a few basic tools. They're inexpensive and can be purchased from most craft or fabric stores.

Embroidery Floss

You'll notice the skeins of floss are color-coded by number, but you won't need to worry about that. I refer to all the colors by name. Of course you can let your imagination roam and use whatever colors you want.

Floss generally comes in six-strand skeins. You'll separate the strands according to the stitch requirements in each project. For most stitches, I like using three or four strands.

Embroidery Needles

These specialized needles have a larger eye than regular sewing needles to accommodate the thicker floss. For the best value, purchase a value pack with multiple sizes. To fight finger fatigue, also look for a rubber needle puller. They're inexpensive and really make embroidering a breeze.

Embroidery Hoop

The hoop keeps the fabric taut for ease of stitching. I prefer plastic hoops because I've found wood hoops tend to snag knit fabric. You can move the hoop as you work to single out your stitch area. Once you get the hang of embroidery, you might find yourself developing personal stitching quirks. For instance, I never use a hoop when I chain stitch.

Transfer Materials

For transferring embroidery patterns, images, and design ideas, you'll need either a pencil, fabric transfer paper, or a water-soluble fabric marker.

If you purchase an embroidery design, follow the manufacturer's instructions for transferring it to your fabric.

A basic sharp pencil works great when you're hand lettering. Transfer paper works best for both simple and detailed designs. Use a water-soluble fabric marker when drawing a design freehand. Pencil marks will come out in the wash. When you follow the manufacturer's instructions for the transfer paper or marker, the lines will disappear once your job is done.

Let's Get Stitching

You'll only need to learn a few basic stitches to create all the designs. As you become more comfortable with embroidery, experiment with new stitches and freehand stitching to create your own designs and patterns.

Straight Stitch or Running Stitch

The stitches can be long or short. A series of straight stitches is called a running stitch.

Backstitch

This stitch creates a solid line of stitches that is perfect for outlining designs.

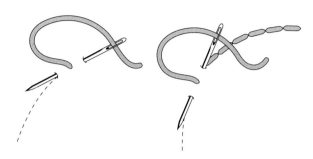

Split Stitch

After you make the first stitch, bring the needle up through the middle of the first stitch to split it. Then continue spitting the stitches as you follow your embroidery line.

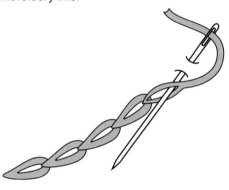

Chain Stitch

This stitch creates a small loop. Use it to stitch a line, or work it in a circle to make a flower.

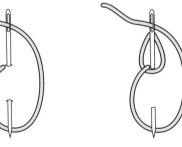

Satin Stitch

The parallel rows of straight stitches made in satin stitch will fill in an outline.

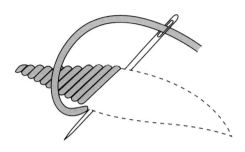

Blanket Stitch

Use the blanket stitch when you want to accentuate an edge. It's a great way to add extra texture.

Whipstitch

Also called the overcast stitch, the whipstitch is used to bind edges. It's perfect for finishing applique.

Q & A

Q: *Will the floss colors bleed when I wash the snapsuit?*

A: I wish I could say no, but the truth is, some colors might bleed. It's best to fix the dye in the floss before using it. You can do this by soaking the floss using a purchased preparation made just for setting dyes.

Q: *How can I organize embroidery floss?*

A: Look for yarn organizers. Winding the floss on small cards keeps it from tangling. Keep the wound skeins in plastic baggies. If you want to get fancy, you can find binders made for storing your embroidery supplies.

Freehand Stitching

With freehand stitching anything goes. Try stitching a series of crisscrossed straight stitches to create little stars, make loops for flowers, or knot the floss as you stitch for polka dots.

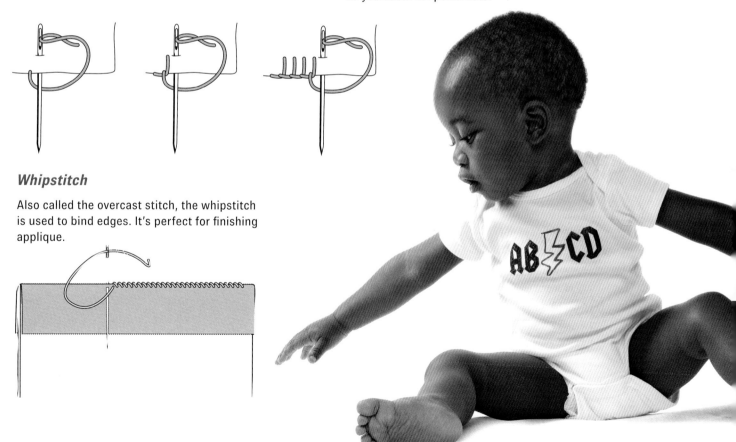

Many different companies and books offer patterns, design ideas, and inspiration for embroidery. For **allover embroidery designs,** try using a combination of patterns; then add your own elements by drawing them freehand.

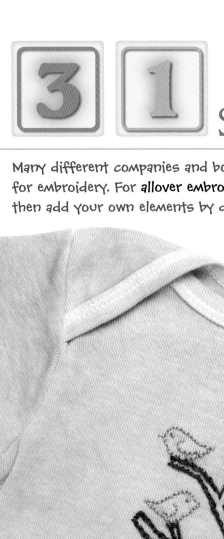

1. Choose a tree design from an embroidery pattern company. Follow the manufacturer's instructions for transferring the design to the front of the snapsuit using transfer paper. If you wish to add your own elements to the design, use a water-soluble fabric marker to draw them freehand.

2. Use an embroidery hoop, embroidery needle, and floss in green, blue, raspberry, and hot pink. For this design, I used a split stitch for the tree and flower stems, a backstitch for the birds, and freehand stitches for the flowers (pages 64 and 65).

TIP: Look for patterns in vintage craft magazines and on antique linens for more inspiration.

D Is for Dog

The **satin stitch** adds dimension to an embroidered design. Use it when you want to fill in an area, like the doggie's eye and nose.

1. Copy the template on page 167, or search for simple clip art of a dog on your computer and print it out. Follow the manufacturer's instructions for transferring the design to the front of the snapsuit using transfer paper. Place the fabric in an embroidery hoop.

2. Thread the needle with six strands of brown embroidery floss. Using the split stitch (page 64), embroider the outline of the dog. Working with six strands of tan embroidery floss, split stitch the mouth or other facial features.

3. Working with six strands of black embroidery floss, split stitch around the eye and nose of the dog. Fill in the eye and nose with the satin stitch (page 65).

Variation
D Is for Darling

Because I'm a jewelry junkie, I knew I needed to incorporate a necklace in a design. Embroidering with the satin stitch lets your little one show off with glitzy flair.

  # Red, White, and Blue

Finish the plain edges of your snapsuit with a **blanket stitch** for a *simple* and *classic* style. This stitch is perfect for adding a decorative touch around a neckline or sleeves.

1. Thread the needle with four strands of blue embroidery floss.

2. Blanket stitch (page 65) over the knit ribbing of the sleeves and neckline.

TIP: Keep the neckline and cuffs comfy by making the stitches loose enough to allow the fabric to stretch when dressing your little one.

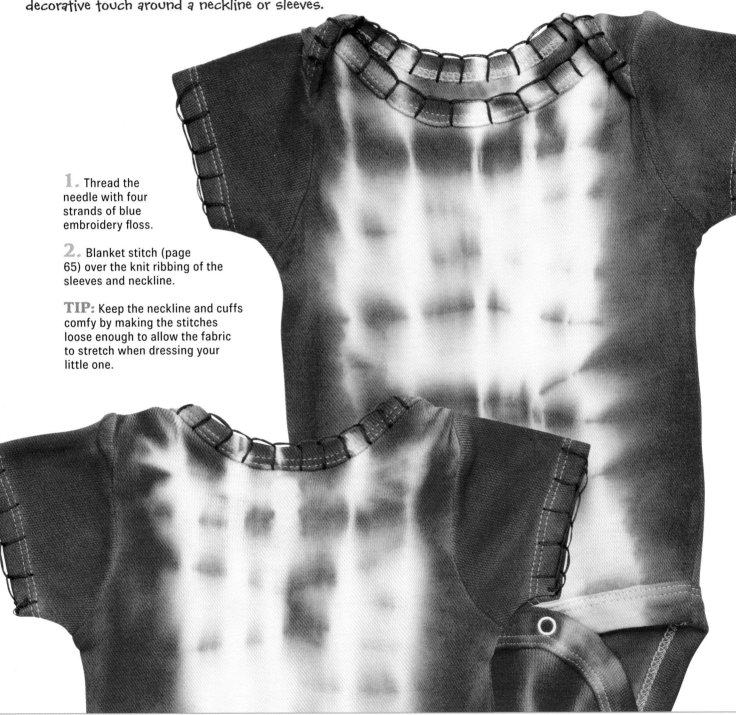

The Future

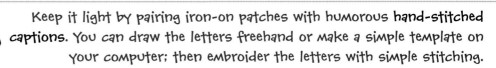

Keep it light by pairing iron-on patches with humorous **hand-stitched** captions. You can draw the letters freehand or make a simple template on your computer; then embroider the letters with simple stitching.

1. Decide where you will place the patch. Use a sharp pencil to draw the letters freehand underneath the area.

2. If you want to make a template, type the words into your computer, adjust the font style and size to your liking, and print it out. Use the template as reference when drawing the letters.

3. Place the snapsuit in an embroidery hoop. Thread a needle with three strands of red embroidery floss. Embroider the letters using the backstitch (page 64).

4. Attach the patch following the manufacturer's instructions. For more information on iron-on patches, visit chapter 6.

  # High Roller

Does your little card shark need some bling? The **chain stitch** is perfect for making faux necklaces, especially when you mix a few strands of metallic floss with regular floss.

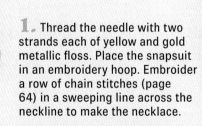

1. Thread the needle with two strands each of yellow and gold metallic floss. Place the snapsuit in an embroidery hoop. Embroider a row of chain stitches (page 64) in a sweeping line across the neckline to make the necklace.

2. Copy the template on page 167. Use it to cut a pendant appliqué from a scrap of gold felt. Position the appliqué at the center of the chain. Attach it to the fabric by using a running stitch or small blanket stitch (pages 64 and 65) around the edges. For more information on appliqué, visit chapter 3.

ABCs Rock

Embroider purchased iron-ons or inkjet transfers for a rockin' double-layer effect. A little embroidery can help highlight select areas or strengthen various design elements such as letters.

1. Center the iron-on, and then follow the manufacturer's instructions for attaching it. For more information on iron-ons and inkjet transfers, visit chapter 6.

2. Thread an embroidery needle with six strands of red embroidery floss. Backstitch (page 64) down the center of the letters.

Variation
Busy Bee

Follow the manufacturer's instructions for affixing a photo transfer to fabric. Thread an embroidery needle with six strands of black floss, and use a split stitch (page 64) to embroider antennas. Attach gathered tulle for the wings.

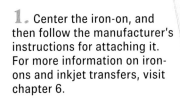

  Sweethearts

Simple **hand-drawn embroidered shapes** can make a big impact. Use a water-soluble fabric marker to create a sweet little freehand design for embroidering.

1. Use a water-soluble fabric marker to draw three small hearts on a tie-dyed snapsuit.

2. Thread an embroidery needle with three strands of raspberry floss. Use a backstitch (page 64) to embroider one of the hearts. Repeat on the remaining hearts, using orange floss for one and peach for the other.

Variation
Space Cadet

Why stop at snapsuits? Tiny embroidered details also look great on cotton baby hats.

Adler

Need to make a cool suit for a little hipster? Look for **mod geometric embroidery designs** on wallpaper, wrapping paper, and fabric. Use floss in three different shades of the same color for a monochromatic color scheme.

1. Copy the template on page 167 or draw, trace, or generate your own design using a computer. Transfer the design to the fabric using transfer paper.

2. Select three different shades of blue floss to use for the design. Place the suit in an embroidery hoop. Thread an embroidery needle with three strands of one blue floss. Embroider over the transferred lines using the backstitch, satin stitch, split stitch, or chain stitch (pages 64 and 65). Change colors as desired.

Tiki Time

Now it's your turn to play with crayons. **Embroider around a melted wax design for a tropical snapsuit fit for your little limbo champ.**

1. Copy the template on page 168. Follow the manufacturer's instructions for transferring the design to fabric using transfer paper.

2. Working on the padded surface of your ironing board, use a brown crayon to color in the rectangle; simple up and down strokes work best.

3. Place a sheet of white paper inside the snapsuit behind the colored rectangle. Place another sheet of paper on top of the colored rectangle. Using a dry iron set at medium-high heat, press the paper to melt the wax and set the color.

4. Thread an embroidery needle with six strands of black floss. Split stitch (page 64) around the edges of the rectangle. Use a variety of stitches to add facial features to the Tiki. While melting the wax, you may lose the transferred lines for the Tiki's features. Refer to the template to guide you as you stitch.

TIP: While I've had success with this technique using many different brands of crayons, you should always test the technique first with the crayons you'll be using.

Tattooed **4 0**

Tired of stitching but still love that hand-sewn look? If so, grab some supplies and **paint an embroidered design** to mimic stitching.

1. Find an image you want to use or copy the template on page 169. If you're looking at clip art, choose a design with simple lines and bold shapes.

2. Trim the image, slip it inside a snapsuit, and tape it to the fabric using low-tack masking tape. You should be able to see the design through the fabric. Light colored suits work best for this technique.

3. Use a detail fabric brush to apply brush-on fabric paint along the outer edges of the design. Make tiny dashes that look like stitches. Allow the paint to dry. Heat set the paint following the manufacturer's instructions.

TIP: For this technique, invest in a fabric paintbrush made especially for detailing. It isn't expensive and allows you to make small painted lines on stretchy cotton knit with ease.

Variation
Flores

Try using iron-ons with an embroidered look. Use one or more to create an allover design.

Chapter 5
Ribbons and Trims

Whether you're creating for a budding baby bohemian or making something for an aspiring Carrie Bradshaw, you can't go wrong adding a dash of ribbon or trim. Incorporate these notions into your designs, or use them to make a simple bow or neck edging.

Ribbons

Ribbons come in many different widths and textures, not to mention their huge variety of prints and colors. You can find ribbons with seasonal themes, stripes, polka dots, and even little rocker guitars.

Grosgrain

Tiny ribbing is the signature of this durable ribbon. Grosgrain is a great choice for decorating kids' clothing because it washes well and is soft and flexible.

Velvet

These plush ribbons require particular care. You don't want the surface to become flattened and shiny, so be sure to use a pressing cloth when ironing.

Satin

Satin ribbons may be single-faced, shiny on one side and dull on the other; or double-faced, shiny on both sides. They make beautiful bows, but they're not very good at disguising baby drool.

Organza

Sheer in appearance, organza ribbons tend to sparkle when the light catches them.

Trim

From ruffled lace to rickrack to crocheted flowers, these trims are in. Use trims that are lightweight, soft, and flexible to avoid scratching baby's delicate skin.

Ruffled Lace

Look for single or double ruffled lace. Single ruffled lace is gathered along one side, creating one ruffled edge. Double ruffled lace is gathered down the center, creating two edges with ruffles.

Rickrack

You can't mistake this zigzag trim for any other. Rickrack is sold in packages and by the yard at most fabric stores.

Crochet and Knit Trims

Buy these by the yard or make your own. Many of the patterns are floral or lacy. Most of them are soft, making them especially suited for decorating a neckline.

Attaching Ribbons and Trim

Attach ribbons and trims by either sewing or gluing them. Whether you're hand or machine stitching, use a ballpoint needle to prevent snagging the knit fabric. If you plan to skip the stitching, there are many different fabric glues on the market. Look for glue that dries soft and crystal clear, is washable, non-toxic, and bonds to fabric, leather, lace, and trim.

Things to Avoid

Do not use wired ribbon, beaded fringe, or heavy trims. The potential for poking and choking hazards mean wires, beads, and babies should never mix. Heavy trims weigh down the fabric, causing the fabric to shift, making it prone to entanglements.

Q & A

Q: *Can I dye ribbon?*

A: Yes, absolutely! Start with a pale shade of cotton or silk ribbon for best results. Cotton laces also dye extremely well.

Sweet Dreams

This little suit is ready for naptime. A thin **trimmed edge** goes a long way toward soft and sweet results.

1. Hand stitch the decorative trim around the neckline.

2. Sew or use fabric glue to attach a little, lightweight sweet dreams patch.

TIP: Take a cue from the colors in your trim. I dyed the snapsuit a pale minty green to match the ribbon.

Variation
So Cute

Cut embroidered floral trim apart to create mini flower patches. Attach them to the snapsuit with a quick stitch or use a drop of fabric glue.

Rock Out

Get ready to rock! Simply attach **themed ribbon**—or use all those little ribbon scraps that haunt your craft bins—to the front of a suit for a bold design.

1. Position the ribbons in a crisscross pattern on the front. Use a small dab of glue from a fabric glue stick to hold them in place.

2. Machine stitch around the edges of each ribbon using a ballpoint needle.

Darling

Add a pop of color to your design with a **simple bow**. It's about the easiest way to transform a plain snapsuit, and with the wide variety of ribbons available, design possibilities are endless.

1. Use a length of ribbon that is 2 inches (5 cm) wide to make a loop. Hand sew the ends together to secure it.

2. With the seam at the back, pinch the center of the loop and wrap it with ribbon that is ½ inch (1.3 cm) wide or less. Sew the wrapped ribbon at the back to hold it in place.

3. Hand sew the bow to the suit. Add a few stitches along the edges of the bow for added security.

TIP: Create a seasonal look with spring print ribbons or show off some holiday glitz with a candy cane stripe.

Variation
Cirque du Bow

Sew a gathering stitch down one long side of 2-inch-wide (5 cm) ribbon. Gather the ribbon until it forms a circle. Sew the center of the circle together as well as the ends. Sew the bow to the snapsuit, and add a pom-pom to the center of the circle, attaching it with a quick stitch or drop of fabric glue.

44 Tushie

Add rows of ruffles to the backside for a cute and sassy look. Gather your own ruffles, or look for soft pre-gathered trims at any fabric store.

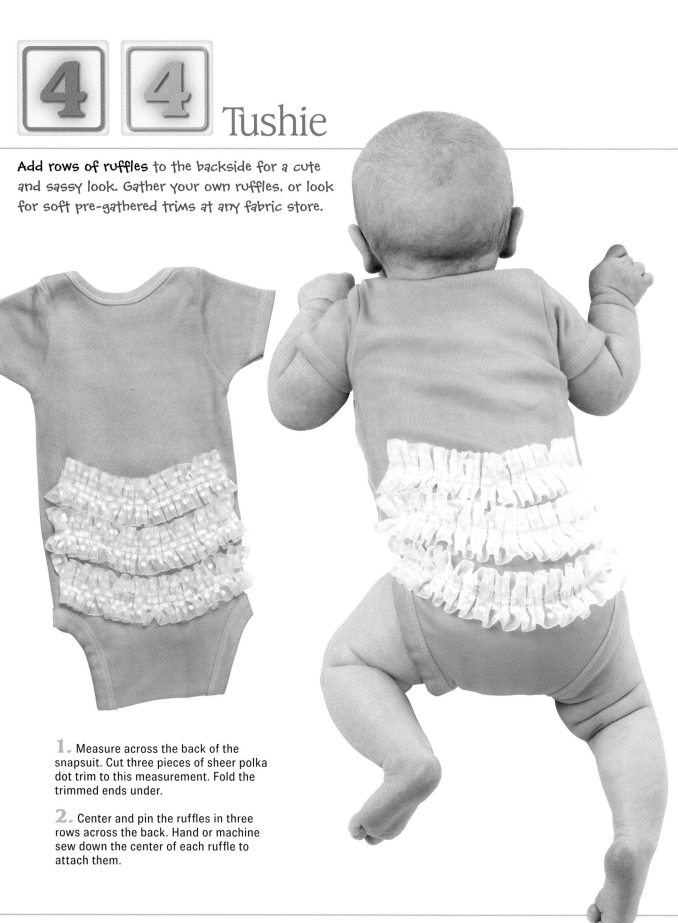

1. Measure across the back of the snapsuit. Cut three pieces of sheer polka dot trim to this measurement. Fold the trimmed ends under.

2. Center and pin the ruffles in three rows across the back. Hand or machine sew down the center of each ruffle to attach them.

Variation
Jr. Prom

It is never too early to start getting ready for the prom! Any little gent will look smashing in this tuxedo-inspired design. You can customize for any color scheme. Imagine a retro olive-green snapsuit with satin ruffles or a soft blush-pink design.

 Prim

Forget the drool, stinky diaper, and mashed peas on her face: your baby can't look anything but prim and proper in this antiqued design, complete with a **lace collar**.

1. Using decorative double lace that is 2 inches (5 cm) wide, cut a length that is 2 inches (5 cm) longer than the neckline on the front.

2. Hand sew a gather stitch along the seamed edge of the lace. Gather the edge to fit the neckline, adjusting the gathers as you go.

3. Hand sew the lace to the suit. Sew or use fabric glue to attach a small flower to the center of the lace at the neckline.

Beachy

What shimmering rhinestone whale wouldn't want to ride forever on blue and green **waves made with ribbon**? This outfit goes with all things beachy.

1. Follow the manufacturer's instructions for attaching the iron-on whale to the top center of the suit. For more information on rhinestone iron-ons, visit chapter 6.

2. Loosely hand gather a small piece of blue and green grosgrain ribbon. Hand sew it underneath the whale. Trim the ends of the ribbon on the diagonal for a neat and nautical finish.

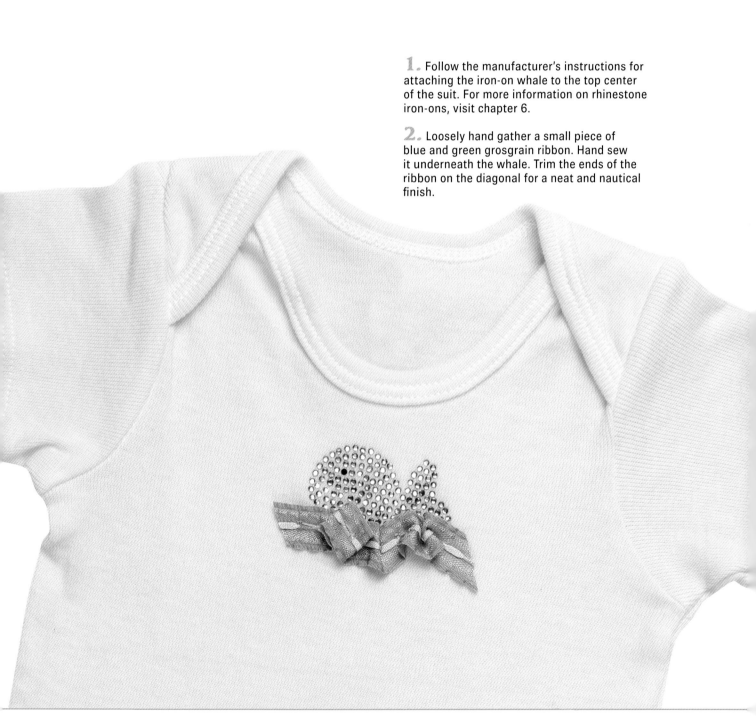

  # Baby Bradshaw

With just a few hand stitches, you can add **ruffled lace sleeves** to make a customized design that'll have your wee one ready for the runway. Look for wide lace that's already gathered.

1. Use a gathered lace trim that is 3 inches (7.6 cm) wide. Starting at the underarm seam and sewing to the back of the sleeve first, stitch the lace to the sleeve seam. Stitch all the way around. If needed, tack the ends of the lace together.

2. Sew a few scraps of lace trim to the back of a ribbon rosette. Secure the rosette to the front by hand sewing through all the layers.

Tulips

Rickrack anyone? Add some sweet personality to felt flower appliqués with **rickrack stems**.

1. Copy the template on page 169. Use it to cut three tulips from hot pink felt.

2. Machine or hand sew three strips of green rickrack in different lengths to the front of the suit.

3. Thread an embroidery needle with orange floss. Sew the tulip appliqués to the tops of their stems using the whipstitch (page 65) around the edges.

Variation
Dainty

Add a small velvet flower to the top center of a snapsuit for an elegant look. Attach it with a quick stitch or a dab of fabric glue, and then highlight the petals with a bit of glitter fabric paint for extra sparkle.

Bohemian

Layering embellishments is key for a boho-inspired design. Try using knit fabric, trim, and patches. Then top it all off with touches of metallic fabric paint.

1. Cut out a motif from a cotton knit print fabric. Leave at least a 1-inch (2.5 cm) allowance around the edges.

2. Cut a piece of lightweight paper-backed fusible web to fit the cutout. Follow the manufacturer's instructions to fuse the webbing to the wrong side of the fabric.

3. Cut out the motif by cutting away the allowance you left in step 1. Remove the paper backing, and place the appliqué in the desired position. Follow the manufacturer's instructions to fuse the appliqué to the snapsuit. If needed, use a pressing cloth over the motif.

4. Using a decorative machine stitch, randomly sew over the knit fabric.

5. Paint a starburst and polka dot design using brush-on metallic taupe fabric paint. Allow to dry.

6. Apply an iron-on feather patch to the suit or attach it using fabric glue. For more about patches, visit chapter 7.

7. Hand sew or machine stitch some velvet trim across the entire design.

Darn Yarn

Don't overlook yarn when thinking about trims. **Textured yarns** almost hide your stitches for you. Just make sure the yarn is easily washable.

1. Form the yarn into your desired shape on the front. Use a fabric glue stick to tack the yarn in place.

2. Hand sew the yarn to the suit. Stitch around the design, making sure your stitches pass through the yarn.

B
A
S
I
C
S

Chapter 6
Iron-Ons

With a few simple techniques (and your iron), you could be finished decorating a snapsuit in the time it takes to make a cup of tea. Look for iron-on letters, premade designs, inkjet transfers, and printable canvas.

Types of Iron-Ons

You'll find many different brands of iron-ons and transfers in retail stores—each with their own set of directions. For best results, always follow the manufacturer's instructions for use.

Start with a washed suit that hasn't been treated with fabric softener. Iron the fabric to remove any wrinkles, but don't use steam. When you're adhering the iron-on, work on a hard, heat-proof surface, and only press it for the recommended time.

Letters

Gone are the days when you could only find letters and numbers in generic fonts. Manufacturers have taken a cue from designer clothing and fashion trends. Today you can find fonts that glitter or resemble tattoos; they can be soft and flocked or embroidered metallics.

Most packages of iron-on letters and numbers contain a few extra. In my experience, plan your design before you go shopping. That way you'll know exactly how many packages you'll need to purchase.

Take time to arrange the letters on the fabric before ironing them in place. To make sure they're evenly spaced, begin with the center letter and work from there. Use a clear ruler to measure the distance between each one. If you want your line of letters to be straight, use a guideline of low-tack masking tape. But be careful when ironing, you don't want to iron over the tape. For a whimsical look, make the letters a bit crooked.

Premade Designs

Many manufacturers offer iron-ons that are specifically designed for baby clothing. They're all cute, so you'll probably have trouble choosing just one. Look for them in craft or fabric shops, or get lost searching the huge inventory you can find online.

Inkjet Transfers

To create a truly personalized design, inkjet transfers are the way to go. An inkjet transfer is really just a specialized paper that you use with your inkjet printer. Basically you can transfer whatever you can print off your computer, like family photos or vintage images. Once you've printed the image, you use an iron to transfer it to your fabric. You can find transfer papers at office supply stores, craft stores, and fabric shops.

Regular transfer paper is perfect when working with white or light-colored clothing. When you're working with dark fabrics, look for transfer paper made especially for them. One downfall to inkjet transfers is that most retail brands will only stand up to about 20 washings.

Printable Canvas

Printable canvas, which has the texture and feel of a lightweight canvas, is designed to go through an inkjet printer. Once you've printed on the canvas, apply iron-on fusible web to the back to create your own iron-on or appliqué.

Alternative Transfer Methods

Crayon wax and laser copy toner are two alternative mediums that will transfer to fabric when heated with an iron. You can buy crayons specifically designed for fabric in the kids' craft section of most craft and fabric stores. Black and white laser copies for transfers can be made at local copy shops or at home if you have the proper equipment.

I like to use a mini iron or heat tool when using these techniques. The mini iron gives you more control over where you apply the heat than with a large iron.

Q & A

Q: *Do you have any washing tips for snapsuits with iron-ons?*

A: Why – yes I do. For best results, launder them inside out in cold water, and hang to dry or tumble dry on low heat.

Team Burp

It's time to stand up for your team! All you need is a package or two of **iron-on letters** to say it loud and proud.

1. Use a clear ruler as a guide to lay out the letters.

2. Follow the manufacturer's instructions to adhere the letters to the snapsuit.

Variation
Party in the Crib

The idea of a party in a crib makes me laugh. Because it's all silliness, position the letters a bit crooked. These iron-on metallic letters mimic the look of embroidery.

Seek and Find

Look closely. Can you find the words MOM, dog, and kiss? Arrange iron-on letters into a word search or use them to create clever patterns and designs.

1. Use a clear ruler to guide you as you lay out the letters in the seek-and-find pattern. Work one row at a time.

2. Follow the manufacturer's instructions for adhering the letters to the front.

Variation

Cyber Bunny

When you work with iron-on letters, you eventually wind up with a bunch of oddballs. Don't toss them. Instead, use them to make new designs. The bunny is made with an O for a head and two Us for ears. Slate-gray embroidery floss for the eyes and nose completes the design.

Stink Happens

Many companies offer adorable iron-ons specifically for baby clothes, including matte designs which have a soft, smooth texture. This **reverse appliqué technique with a matte iron-on** creates a fabric frame for the revealed image.

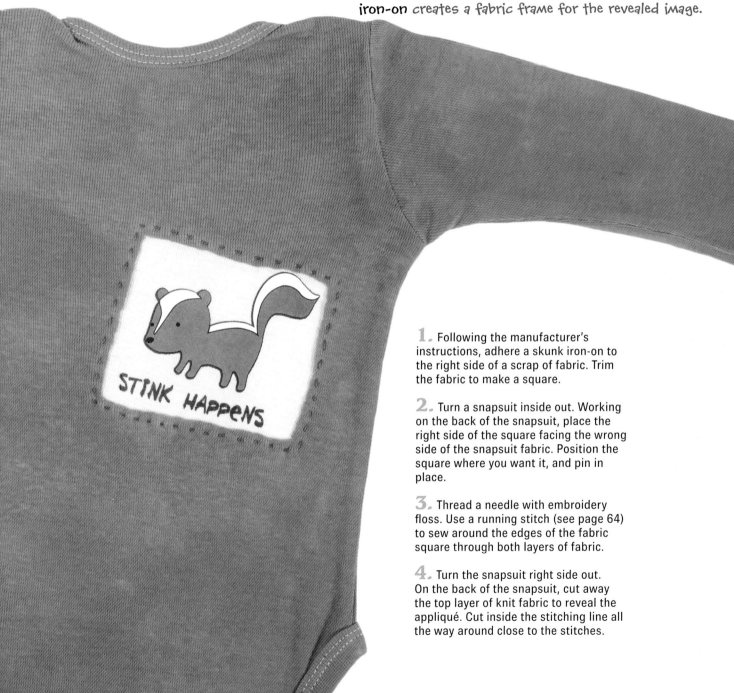

1. Following the manufacturer's instructions, adhere a skunk iron-on to the right side of a scrap of fabric. Trim the fabric to make a square.

2. Turn a snapsuit inside out. Working on the back of the snapsuit, place the right side of the square facing the wrong side of the snapsuit fabric. Position the square where you want it, and pin in place.

3. Thread a needle with embroidery floss. Use a running stitch (see page 64) to sew around the edges of the fabric square through both layers of fabric.

4. Turn the snapsuit right side out. On the back of the snapsuit, cut away the top layer of knit fabric to reveal the appliqué. Cut inside the stitching line all the way around close to the stitches.

Love

Flocked iron-ons are soft and fuzzy and meant to be touched. Though their intricate lines make them look delicate, they hold up surprisingly well through many washings.

1. Layer two different flocked iron-ons to create one look.

2. Place the iron-ons in the desired position on the front. Follow the manufacturer's instructions for adhering them to the fabric.

Variation
Butter Bum

Designs don't always have to be front and center. Backsides need a little decorating now and then. This is a great way to cover a stain.

Variation
Amy

Soft flocked letters are particularly cute when they spell out a little girl's name. Look for letters that have flowers or hearts cut into the design.

  Glitter Love

Glittery iron-ons remind me of the T-shirts I used to wear roller skating under a disco ball in the 1970s. They're perfect for a retro look that sparkles.

1. On the front of the snapsuit, center a glittered heart iron-on.

2. Follow the manufacturer's instructions for adhering the iron-on to the fabric.

Variation
Goth

Combine glitter gothic letters and a flocked skull iron-on to create a truly underground look.

Use **dark fabric inkjet transfers** when working with darker fabrics. If you use regular transfers, which are clear, the dark fabric will show right through the design.

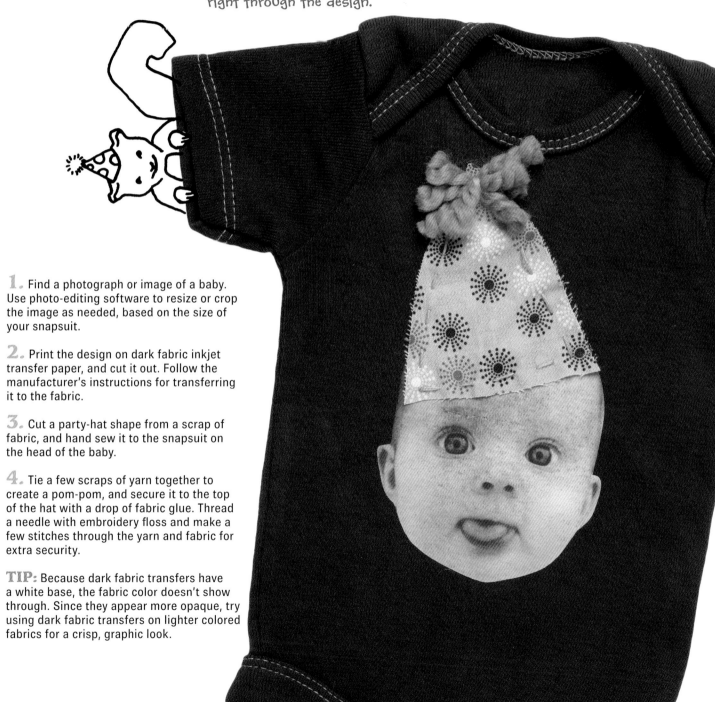

1. Find a photograph or image of a baby. Use photo-editing software to resize or crop the image as needed, based on the size of your snapsuit.

2. Print the design on dark fabric inkjet transfer paper, and cut it out. Follow the manufacturer's instructions for transferring it to the fabric.

3. Cut a party-hat shape from a scrap of fabric, and hand sew it to the snapsuit on the head of the baby.

4. Tie a few scraps of yarn together to create a pom-pom, and secure it to the top of the hat with a drop of fabric glue. Thread a needle with embroidery floss and make a few stitches through the yarn and fabric for extra security.

TIP: Because dark fabric transfers have a white base, the fabric color doesn't show through. Since they appear more opaque, try using dark fabric transfers on lighter colored fabrics for a crisp, graphic look.

  # Rap Music

Create your own iron-on design! Find a digital image or scan one into your computer, print it out on inkjet transfer paper, and you're ready to get creative.

1. Find an image of a cassette tape. Use photo-editing software to resize or crop the image as needed, based on the size of your snapsuit. If the image has words, flip it to get a mirror image so the words come out correctly when printed.

2. Print the design on inkjet transfer paper, and cut it out. Follow the manufacturer's instructions for transferring it to the fabric.

TIP: Try printing several small images on one sheet; then cut them out to make different designs.

Variation
Stars and Stripes

Use inkjet transfers to make designs that coordinate with a particular suit. Print them in a shade similar to the dyed fabric for a cool and subtle look.

Variation
Dirty Diaper Dancing

Generate pop-culture text on your computer and print it out when you want a add touch of humor. This classic line from the movie *Dirty Dancing* seems made for a snapsuit.

nobody puts **BABY** in a corner

Here

To create a transfer with the look and feel of printed fabric, use **inkjet printable canvas**. Retail shops sell a variety of weights and brands.

1. Use your computer and inkjet printer to print an image of a map on printable canvas. Heat set the design.

2. Attach a piece of paper-backed fusible web to the back of the printed map. Cut around the map, leaving a small border of the fusible web around the design. Center the map on the snapsuit, remove the paper, and follow the manufacturer's instructions for adhering it to the fabric.

3. Use a straight stitch or zigzag on your sewing machine to sew around the edges of the map.

4. Cut a small arrow from a scrap of felt. Place it where you want it, and attach it with fabric glue. For extra security, hand sew it to the fabric.

Variation
Pretty as a Picture

Silhouettes are always in style. Alter a photo using photo-editing software to make it into a silhouette. Print it on the canvas, and attach it using paper-backed fusible web. Frame the design in gold trim.

Variation
Altered

Vintage photos or mini-collages look wonderful when printed on canvas. Attach the elements using paper-backed fusible web. Add some additional details like flower petals, glitter, or ribbon to make altered art.

  # Robbie

Capture the art of an older sibling with a **crayon iron-on transfer**. This technique is fun for the whole family, and kids enjoy helping to design clothes for the baby.

1. Use fabric transfer crayons to draw a design on white paper. If you want to use the drawing of the robot, copy the template on page 170. Press hard while drawing. Brush away any loose specks of wax.

2. Place a piece of white paper inside the snapsuit to prevent the color from seeping through.

3. Lay the drawing, colored side down, on the snapsuit in the desired position. Press the paper with a hot iron, no steam. Press and hold as you iron for one or two minutes. Try not to move the paper as you press.

4. Carefully remove the paper. Launder in cold water, and hang to dry.

TIP: If you're using text in your design, remember to draw it in reverse so it will read correctly when transferred.

Crowned

Create a **laser toner copy transfer** for a fashionable design that comes with a pre-faded, worn look a la designer jeans. If you don't have a laser printer at home, try a local copy shop.

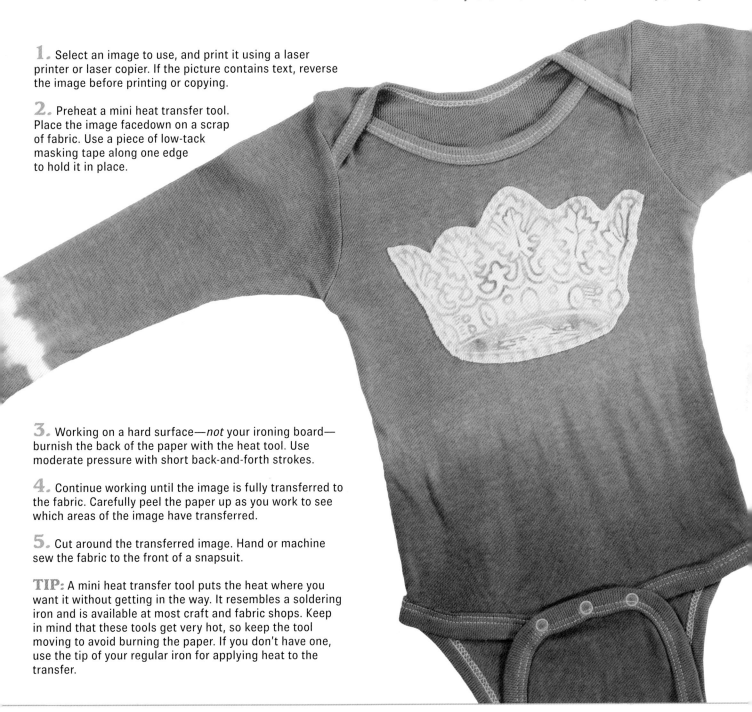

1. Select an image to use, and print it using a laser printer or laser copier. If the picture contains text, reverse the image before printing or copying.

2. Preheat a mini heat transfer tool. Place the image facedown on a scrap of fabric. Use a piece of low-tack masking tape along one edge to hold it in place.

3. Working on a hard surface—*not* your ironing board—burnish the back of the paper with the heat tool. Use moderate pressure with short back-and-forth strokes.

4. Continue working until the image is fully transferred to the fabric. Carefully peel the paper up as you work to see which areas of the image have transferred.

5. Cut around the transferred image. Hand or machine sew the fabric to the front of a snapsuit.

TIP: A mini heat transfer tool puts the heat where you want it without getting in the way. It resembles a soldering iron and is available at most craft and fabric shops. Keep in mind that these tools get very hot, so keep the tool moving to avoid burning the paper. If you don't have one, use the tip of your regular iron for applying heat to the transfer.

Chapter 7
Patches

How can such a small item have so much design impact? Patches offer endless inspiration for embellishing snapsuits. Look for them in fabric and craft shops. If your tastes run more retro, look into vintage shops and online auctions where some amazing finds can be made.

All About Patches

If you want to create a custom patch, make your own using inkjet printable fabrics, felt, or fleece. Keep in mind that not all patches have to be patches. Woven labels and crocheted flowers can also serve the purpose.

Evaluate each patch you're considering to make sure it's baby safe. Check the edges for any loose threads that might have sharp edges due to glue or sizing. If a patch is stiff, try bending it back and forth to make it more pliable. You can also soak it in hot water to remove some of the sizing.

Large patches may be too heavy for the knit fabric. Small to medium size patches are best suited for baby clothing because they're lightweight.

Attaching Patches

Most patches available in retail stores are iron-ons; all you need is a household iron to attach them. Follow the manufacturer's instructions for adhering them, and you can't go wrong.

Generally, attaching them follows a simple process. First, place the patch glue side down in the desired position. Then place a pressing cloth over the patch, and iron, using firm pressure. Next, turn the suit inside out, and iron the back of the patch. Finally, for extra security, you can use a needle and thread to hand tack the edges of the patch to the fabric.

To attach vintage patches and those that aren't self adhesive, sew around the edges using a coordinating thread. Most patches have a seamed edge that's easy to sew through and makes the stitches virtually undetectable. For larger patches, use a fabric glue stick to hold the patch in place while stitching.

Fabric glues provide a quick and easy way to attach a patch. When using the glue method on baby clothing, it's best to add a few stitches around the edges of the patch for extra security.

Q: *Can I repurpose patches?*

A: If you love a patch that's attached to a snapsuit that's past its prime, or if your little one has grown out of it, you can easily cut around the patch and reuse it for a new design.

Vegas Baby

Got a mean poker face? This ultra-quick design idea—with a **purchased patch front and center**—works well for medium- to large-sized patches.

1. Center the patch on the front of the suit.

2. If the patch is an iron-on, follow the manufacturer's instructions for adhering it. If not, use fabric glue or hand stitch to attach.

Variation
Pink Pirate

Iridescent or glitzy patches make the best girly designs. Iridescent patches show off their soft multicolor shimmer when the light hits them just right.

 Future Sailor

Changing the placement of patches can add interest to Your design... and make sure baby looks couture from every angle. The shoulder, back, and sleeve are all good choices for featuring a patch design.

1. Iron the sleeve flat. Center an anchor patch on the sleeve.

2. If the patch is an iron-on, follow the manufacturer's instructions for adhering it. If not, use fabric glue or hand stitch to attach. For an iron-on or glued patch, hand sew around the edge for extra security.

3. Use iron-on letters to spell FUTURE SAILOR. For more info on iron-on letters, visit chapter 6.

TIP: When attaching patches to a sleeve, hand sew around the patch after ironing or gluing to prevent the edges from popping up after washings.

Variation
Fruity

Hats off to patches! Mini patches add a small design detail to the brim of a cotton cap.

Variation
Chick a Dee

Create a design with multiple minis. Attach a cluster of small patches near the top shoulder area for a quick and cute treatment.

Fast Eddie

Using **name patches** is a perfect way to personalize a design. Look for patches at vintage clothing and collectable shops. Otherwise, you can find them at craft and fabric stores as well as online.

1. Center the patch on the suit.

2. If the patch is an iron-on, follow the manufacturer's instructions for adhering it. If not, use fabric glue or hand stitch to attach. For an iron-on or glued patch, hand sew around the edge for extra security.

TIP: If you're looking for a customized name patch, go to a mall kiosk that embroiders clothing or to a uniform supply store.

Blue Bird

If you want a 3-D effect, **layer patches** over inkjet transfers, painted designs, or tie-dyed patterns. Always glue or hand sew a patch over an inkjet transfer. If you use an iron-on patch, the heat from the iron will melt the transfer: what a mess!

1. Create and transfer an inkjet transfer of a crown to the suit. For more info on inkjet transfers, visit chapter 6.

2. Lay a bird patch that resembles a tattoo over the transfer, and attach by hand sewing or gluing.

3. Add some glitz by gluing rhinestones around the design. Use glue made for attaching gems to fabric.

Major Poop

Creating your own fabric patch with inkjet printable fabric is an easy way to create a custom design. Use word processing or photo-editing software to design a patch or scan a patch and alter it as you wish.

1. Center a distressed military-themed iron-on on the front. Follow the manufacturer's instructions for adhering it to the suit.

2. Glue a few star-shaped studs around or on the patch. Use glue made for attaching gems to fabric.

3. Create and heat set an inkjet transfer on printable fabric that reads MAJOR POOP in army green. For more on inkjet transfers, visit chapter 6.

4. Center the patch and attach it by sewing around the edges.

TIP: Printable fabrics are available online and at craft or fabric retailers. There are several different brands on the market and each brand will have their own set of detailed instructions. Be sure to follow the manufacturer's instructions when creating your patch.

Variation
Stinker

After printing the patch, and prior to cutting it out, fuse a piece of paper-backed fusible web to the back of the fabric. Cut out the patch, and you're ready to attach it. For a more permanent design, sew around the outer edge of the patch.

Star

Like felting wool, **ironing fleece** on high heat—something you usually want to avoid—will flatten the pile, resulting in a denser fleece patch with plenty of huggable, lovable texture.

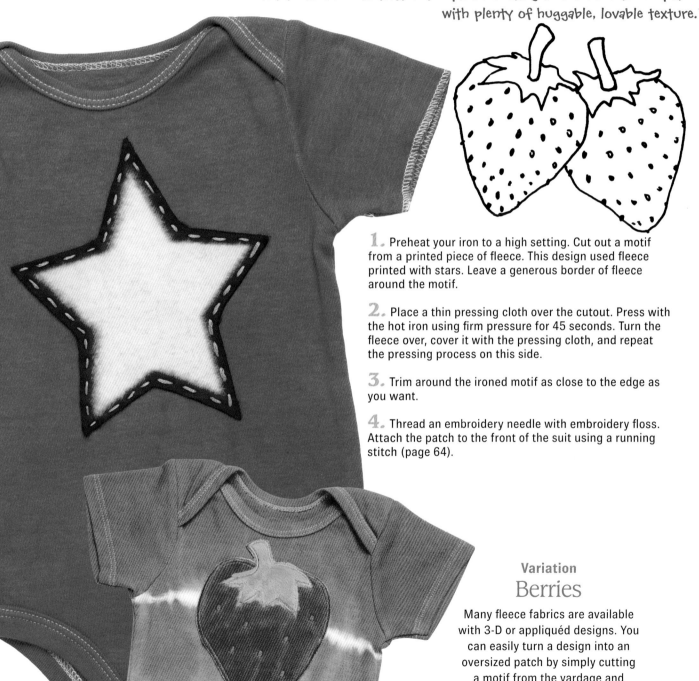

1. Preheat your iron to a high setting. Cut out a motif from a printed piece of fleece. This design used fleece printed with stars. Leave a generous border of fleece around the motif.

2. Place a thin pressing cloth over the cutout. Press with the hot iron using firm pressure for 45 seconds. Turn the fleece over, cover it with the pressing cloth, and repeat the pressing process on this side.

3. Trim around the ironed motif as close to the edge as you want.

4. Thread an embroidery needle with embroidery floss. Attach the patch to the front of the suit using a running stitch (page 64).

Variation
Berries

Many fleece fabrics are available with 3-D or appliquéd designs. You can easily turn a design into an oversized patch by simply cutting a motif from the yardage and sewing it to a snapsuit.

  # Squirrel Power

Felt patches are wonderfully touchable and easy to make. This squirrel patch was made by copying and enlarging the foam stamp I used to create the background design.

1. Place a foam stamp on a photocopier or scanner, and enlarge it to your desired size. Use it as a pattern to cut the design from a piece of light brown felt. Set it aside.

2. Apply brown brush-on fabric paint to the foam stamp using a foam paintbrush. Stamp the image in several spots on the front to create an overall design. Allow to dry, and heat set the paint following the manufacturer's instructions.

3. Center the felt cutout on the front. Thread an embroidery needle with brown embroidery floss, and attach the patch using a running stitch (page 64). Use blue embroidery floss to embroider an eye.

TIP: If you want to take a shortcut, copy the template on page 170 and use it to cut out the squirrel from felt. Use a small squirrel or acorn stamp with brown brush-on fabric paint to print your overall design.

Made with Love

Iron-on woven labels make great patches. You can pick up "made by" labels at fabric stores that feature common names, or, for the ultimate in designer fashion, have custom labels inexpensively printed online.

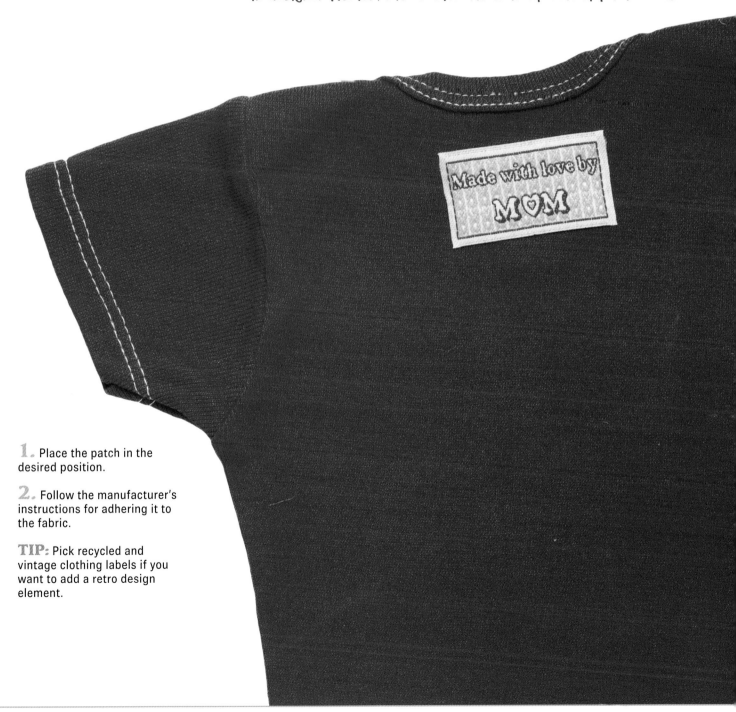

1. Place the patch in the desired position.

2. Follow the manufacturer's instructions for adhering it to the fabric.

TIP: Pick recycled and vintage clothing labels if you want to add a retro design element.

  # Sunny Flowers

If you crochet or knit, you can create little **flower or doily patches** in no time. Better yet, enlist a crafty family member to contribute to the design.

1. Slip a piece of waxed paper inside the suit to prevent the glue from seeping through. Add a drop of fabric glue to the center back of each patch, and place them on the front as desired. Allow to dry.

2. Hand sew the edges and/or petals with coordinating threads to secure.

TIP: For extra design detail, plan ahead when dyeing the suit by tie-dyeing circles (page 20) to frame the flowers.

Indulge in some word play for your design. Combine iron-on letters and picture patches to complete a catchy phrase.

1. Attach an owl patch to a snapsuit. If the patch is an iron-on, follow the manufacturer's instructions for adhering it. If not, use fabric glue or hand stitch to attach. For an iron-on or glued patch, hand sew around the edge for extra security.

2. Line up the letters to spell NIGHT across the top of the owl. Follow the manufacturer's instructions for adhering the letters to the fabric.

TIP: At a loss for words? Phrases like night owl, be (bee) happy, bad apple, cry baby, funny bunny, sweet pea, or lucky duck can be made by combining words with patches.

Variation
Bee Happy

If you're stumped for color ideas when dyeing a suit, use your design elements as inspiration. For this project, I used two different yellows to coordinate with the bee patch.

Chapter 8

Cut, Ripped, Torn

When I was a teenager in the 1980s, if your clothes weren't torn, you weren't hip! Now that the style is hot again, your snapsuit design can be just as cool with a few simple snips of the scissors.

Tools

Scissors, scissors, and more scissors. You've probably guessed by now that the main tools for making the designs in this chapter are scissors. You can find the many different sizes and shapes needed at craft and fabric stores.

Sewing Shears

Think sharp when it comes to your sewing shears. Never use them on paper, and always store them in their sheath. I label my shears FABRIC ONLY with a permanent marker just in case my hubby picks them up. Maintain your sewing shears with regular sharpening, and they'll always be ready for action.

Fine-Tipped Scissors

These small scissors are a must for anyone working on baby clothes. You can use them to cut close to seams, pierce holes, or make fringe. Maintain them as you would your sewing shears—don't use them on paper, sharpen regularly, and store them in their sheath.

Pinking Shears

The serrated edge on pinking shears is meant to trim fabric to prevent fraying. But the zigzag cut they make is irresistible for decorating an edge.

Decorative-Edge Scissors

If you're cutting anyway, you might as well make a decorative edge. You can find decorative scissors in many styles, like scallop shears and wave scissors. Make sure you use scissors that are made for cutting fabric and not for scrapbooking.

Techniques

Cut, snip, clip, and trim. It's that easy. The projects in this chapter offer several ideas for decorating snapsuits using scissors. Once you feel comfortable with the idea, I urge you to experiment with your own designs and cutting methods to create new looks.

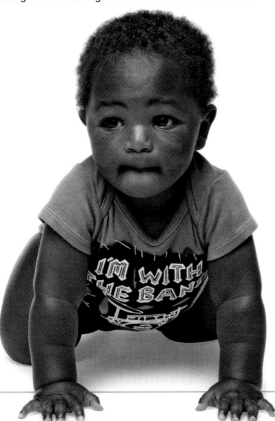

Q & A

Q: *What's the best way to sharpen scissors?*

A: You can use a home sharpener, but my best advice is to have a professional do the sharpening. Most fabric stores offer this service once a month. The price is nominal in exchange for years of happy cutting.

7 1 Pinked

Jazz up a snapsuit by transforming it into a baby T-shirt. When you use **pinking shears** or other decorative-edge scissors, it only takes a minute to get a new look.

1. Use pinking shears to cut across the snapsuit below the waist through both layers of fabric.

2. Remove the sleeve bands by using the pinking shears to cut through both layers of fabric on each sleeve just above the stitching line.

Variation
Petals

Cut the snapsuit as you did for Pinked, but use scalloped shears for a soft, feminine edge. Accent the design by sewing on a few silk petals to make a flower, then attach a pearl in the center of it. If you glue the pearl, use glue made for attaching gems to fabric.

Variation
Save the Wave

Wave shears create a long wave pattern. Cut the suit at the waist but leave the sleeves intact. Add an iron-on patch with the recycling logo to the center of the shirt. For more information on iron-ons, visit chapter 6.

Kirigami

Both punky and spunky, this design will cool baby on hot summer days. Use scissors to **make little cuts to outline a design,** such as this heart shape that magically appears.

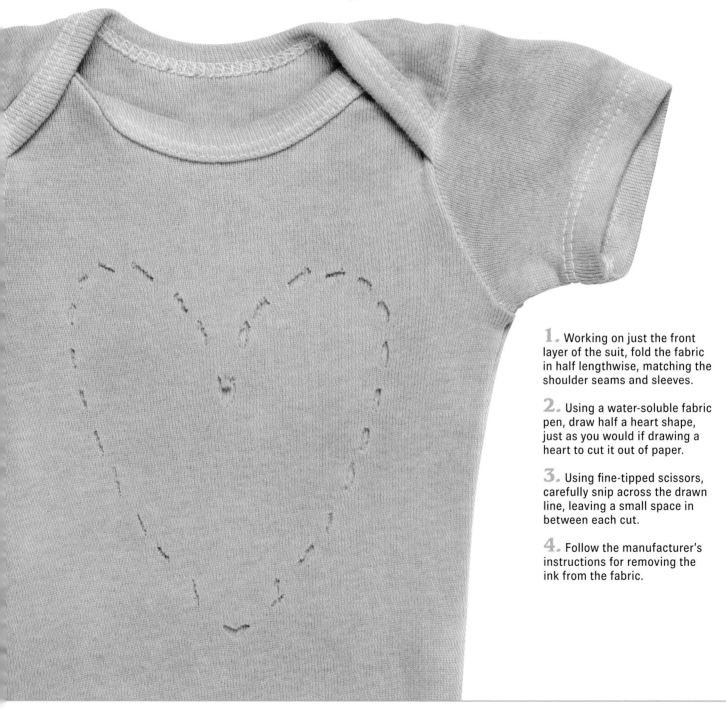

1. Working on just the front layer of the suit, fold the fabric in half lengthwise, matching the shoulder seams and sleeves.

2. Using a water-soluble fabric pen, draw half a heart shape, just as you would if drawing a heart to cut it out of paper.

3. Using fine-tipped scissors, carefully snip across the drawn line, leaving a small space in between each cut.

4. Follow the manufacturer's instructions for removing the ink from the fabric.

Venice Boardwalk

From the retro-fabulous airbrush design to the funky cut fringe, this design captures the laid-back feel of life at water's edge.... plus a few hearts along the way.

1. Remove the sleeve bands by using sewing shears to cut through both layers of fabric on each sleeve just above the stitching line. Use fine-tipped scissors to fringe the sleeves, cutting only up to the shoulder seam.

2. Cut off the bottom of the suit, turning it into a T-shirt. Fringe the bottom of the shirt using the fine-tipped scissors.

3. Find an airbrushed design online, or scan one you like. Use it to make an iron-on transfer by printing it on inkjet transfer paper. Follow the manufacturer's instructions for transferring it to the front. For more information on inkjet transfers, visit chapter 6.

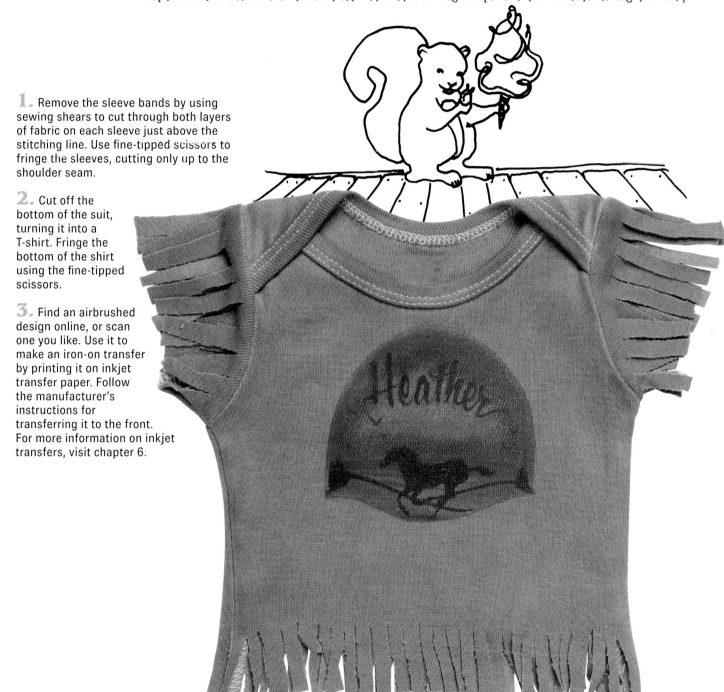

  # Tiny Dancer

With a few **snips, stitches, and some pink tulle,** your little ballerina can have her own tutu in less than an hour.

1. Working close to the shoulder seam, cut off the sleeves, and fold the excess fabric under. Thread a needle with pink embroidery floss. Sew the fabric flat to the shoulder seam. Try using the blanket stitch (page 65) or whipstitch (page 65). Alternate long and short stitches for an artistic look, or sew even stitches for a more polished look.

2. Cut off the neck binding from the front of the snapsuit only. Use embroidery floss to add a decorative running stitch (page 64) around the front neckline.

3. From ½ yard (45.7 cm) of pink tulle, cut two strips, each 8 inches (20.3 cm) long and the entire width of the fabric. Layer the two strips on top of each other, and hand gather along one edge.

4. Working on just the front, use a water-soluble fabric pen to mark a line just below the waist. Hand sew the gathered tulle along the marked line.

5. Hand sew or glue embellishments to the tutu. Embellishments could include silk flowers, ribbons, rhinestones, sequins, and lace. When attaching rhinestones, sequins, or gems, use glue made for attaching gems to fabric.

The Drools

The Drools rule! This super cool snapsuit, cut off and embellished with an inkjet transfer, is a cinch to make with scissors and simple photo-editing software.

1. Cutting close to the shoulder seam line, cut off the sleeves.

2. Cut off the bottom of the suit, turning it into a T-shirt.

3. Find a picture of a record album online, or scan one you like. Use photo-editing software to color it, and to title the album The Drools.

4. Use the image to make an iron-on transfer by printing it on inkjet transfer paper. Follow the manufacturer's instructions for transferring it. For more information on inkjet transfers, visit chapter 6.

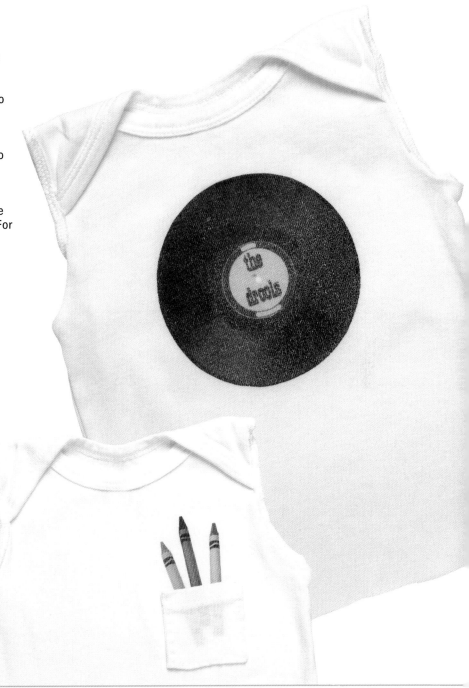

Variation
Cool Nerd

Create an inkjet transfer of crayons, and follow the manufacturer's instructions for transferring it to the front of the snapsuit. Cut off the sleeves, and use one to make a little pocket. Hand or machine sew the pocket over the image with the crayons poking out.

  # Say Cheese

Hold your nose, because this holey Swiss-cheese-inspired design is as stinky as it gets! Be prepared for lots of smiles when your little one dons this design, created by cutting holes in a snapsuit.

stinky

1. Apply iron-on letters that spell stinky across the front. For more information on iron-on letters, visit chapter 6.

2. Cutting through both layers of fabric, use fine-tipped scissors to cut random holes in various sizes all over the snapsuit.

Variation
Peek-a-Boo Polka Dots

Peek-a-boo, I tickle you! The openings cut into the dots are perfect for tickling babies. Use a bleach pen (page 24) to make dots of various sizes on the front of a dyed suit. Cut an X in the center of each dot.

  # My Daddy Rocks

Go for a real edgy look with **free-form appliqué**. Cut a rock-n-roll motif design from an old T-shirt, then cut slices from the center to highlight the appliqué.

1. Cut out a rock-and-roll motif from an old, clean T-shirt. Leave at least a 1-inch (2.5 cm) allowance around the edges.

2. Cut a piece of lightweight paper-backed fusible web to fit the cutout. Follow the manufacturer's instructions to fuse the webbing to the wrong side of the fabric.

3. Cut out the motif by cutting around it in a free-form style. Keep as much or as little of the allowance left in step 1 as you want. Cut slices from the center of the design.

4. Remove the paper backing, and place the appliqué in the desired position. Follow the manufacturer's instructions to fuse the appliqué to the snapsuit. If needed, use a pressing cloth over the motif.

5. Sew around the appliqué, combining hand-sewn stitches with machine stitching. Use different color threads, and mix up the stitches for an even bigger, bolder look.

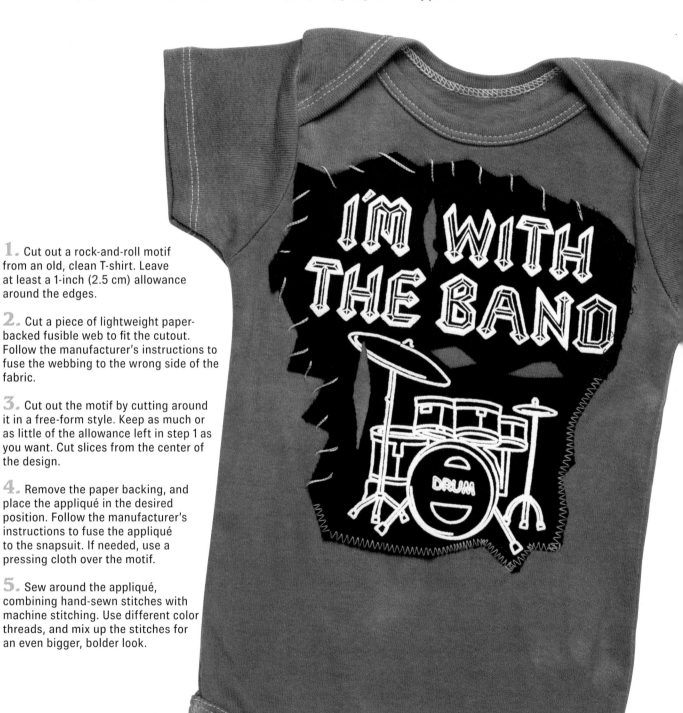

Sunday Drive

It pays to recycle when you re-craft. This **conjoined technique** works well if you have two suits with stains or snags but in otherwise good condition.

1. Start with two different colored snapsuits. Working through both layers, cut one of the suits off just above the waistline, and then cut the other one off just below the waistline.

2. Thread an embroidery needle with embroidery floss. Overlap the top with the bottom and hand sew them together using a running stitch (page 64).

3. Make an appliqué from a scrap of cotton fabric and the template on page 171, or attach an iron-on patch. For more information on appliqué, visit chapter 3; for more information on iron-ons, visit chapter 6.

TIP: The quick and easy running stitch is soft on baby bellies and allows for lots of stretch.

Janis

If you can tie a shoe, you can easily create this long-sleeve snapsuit with **lace-up sleeves**. Dye the suit in contrasting colors, and choose a ribbon that matches one of them.

1. Tie-dye a long sleeve snapsuit using the marbled technique on page 22. Allow to dry.

2. Fold the sleeves flat, and cut them at an angle with the longest point at the underarm seam.

3. Keeping the sleeve flat, and working through *both* layers of the fabric, use a sharp, fine-tipped scissors to pierce three holes in one of the sleeves along the top fold. Make the first hole ½ inch (1.3 cm) in from the edge of the sleeve, then evenly space the remaining two holes.

4. Open the sleeve. You should have six side-by-side holes. Thread a length of ribbon through the sleeve like a shoelace, and tie a bow. Sew the bow in position with a needle and thread for safety. Repeat steps 3 and 4 on the other sleeve.

5. For an extra design element, apply an iron-on to the front. For more information on iron-ons, visit chapter 6.

TIP: For this design, I used turquoise and red dye for the marbled technique.

Dustie

Transform your dyeing mishaps into something wonderful. The pink and brown fabrics used to create this project came from dyeing disasters.

1. Cutting as close to the shoulder seams as possible, cut off the sleeves from a mistake snapsuit. Make a line of long running stitches ¼ inch (6 mm) in from the edge across the top of each cut sleeve. Use the stitches to gather the sleeves. Sew them to the shoulder seams of a good suit. Cut the armbands off both sleeves of the good snapsuit.

2. Cut a small strip of fabric from another mistake snapsuit or from a scrap of fabric. Use dimensional fabric paint in a pearl color to add a row of pearls down the center of the strip. Allow to dry. Use fine-tipped scissors to cut a hole in the center of the strip.

3. Cut three rough-edge circles for the flower petals. Cut one large and one small from the mistake snapsuit used for the sleeves. Cut a medium circle from the same fabric used for the strip in step 2.

4. Decide where you want to place the center of the flower on the good snapsuit. Use the fine-tipped scissors to cut two holes on either side of this point. Thread a ¾-yard (68.6 cm) length of soft sheer ribbon through the holes.

5. Cut two small holes in the center of each circle to correspond with the holes you cut in the snapsuit. Thread the circles from largest to smallest onto the ribbon.

6. To finish, thread both ends of the ribbon through the hole in the pearled strip. Tie a secure knot in the ribbon, followed by a bow. Trim the ends of the ribbon to the desired length.

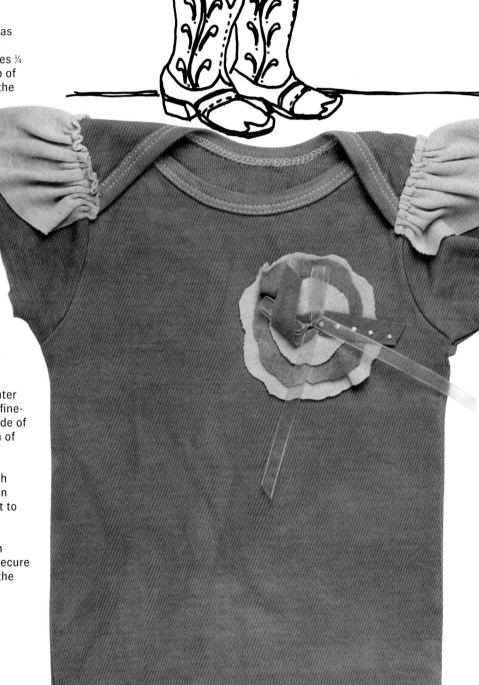

Chapter 9

Bring on the Bling

You're never too young for glitzy glamour—not even a newborn! Baby girls—and boys—sparkle when you decorate their snapsuits with a bit of bling.

Bling, Bling, and More Bling

I don't know where my love of sparkly clothes came from. Perhaps it was our Moroccan neighbor with her shimmering headscarves, or it could have been the rhinestones on the Rockettes' costumes. I'm just glad I haven't lost my fascination with all that glitters. Today, there are so many options for bringing on the bling, I don't know where to start.

Iron-ons

Looking to whip up a quick design? Try iron-ons featuring rhinestones, studs, and foil transfers.

Look for a variety of bejeweled designs including those with words, hearts, skulls, team logos, animals, tattoos, and flowers. You can also buy iron-on rhinestones and studs loose for making your own

designs. Look for foil transfer material in sheets for cutting your own custom shapes or when you want to create a shiny background.

When you attach iron-on rhinestones and studs, carefully follow the manufacturer's instructions. If you use too much or too little heat, your stones will not adhere properly.

Loose Rhinestones

Use loose rhinestones to bring a pop of color and shimmer to any design. Purchase them at local craft and fabric stores or online. I've found online retailers carry the widest selection.

Look for flat-backed stones that are made of crystal or acrylic. Crystal stones feature a brilliant shine and are the most expensive. Acrylic stones are less expensive and are slightly less shiny than crystal stones. Both work equally well. Stones are available in every color and have different finishes. Rhinestones marked AB (aurora borealis) have a rainbow effect, and those marked SC have special coatings or cuts.

Stones come in different sizes measured in millimeters, the smallest being 1.8mm and the largest 35mm, roughly the size of a quarter. You can find rounds, squares, tear drops, hearts, emerald cuts, and even specialty shapes.

Don't use a rhinestone-setting tool to attach loose rhinestones to a snapsuit. A setter can leave sharp edges that are not very baby friendly. Instead, glue them using glue that's suitable for adhering gems to fabric. The glue should be non-toxic, washable, and designed for adhering porous and semi-porous surfaces together. A little glue goes a long way, so don't buy the giant economy size.

Patches

Patches made with metallic threads bring the bling with little effort and expense.

Depending on the type of patch you're using, you'll either hand or machine sew it to the suit, iron it on, or attach it with glue.

Select patches that are light or medium weight. Heavy patches can pull and twist knit fabric. Check the patches to make sure they don't have sharp edges. If you're looking for an unusual or vintage design, search online auctions and specialized retail-craft websites.

Paints

Metallic, pearl, and glitter fabric paints add excitement to your designs.

When working with paints, be sure to tuck a piece of waxed paper inside the suit. This simple step prevents the paint from seeping to the other side. Since fabric paints need to be heat set prior to laundering, follow the manufacturer's instructions. Look for their care guidelines as well.

Q: *What's the best way to store loose rhinestones?*

A: I store my loose stones in clear plastic divider boxes sorted by color and size. I keep tiny rhinestones in little zip top bags.

Q: *How can I prevent glue from seeping around the edges of the stones?*

A: Apply the glue with the head of a straight pin to prevent using too much of it. Place a small amount of glue on a piece of waxed paper, dip the head of the pin into it, and then dot the glue onto the fabric in the desired position. Attach your rhinestone, and allow the glue to dry. Goodbye glue globs!

Anchors Away

The patch aisle at the fabric store can be a dangerous place for your pocketbook, especially if you're attracted to sparkly things like I am. When I saw this sailing-themed **metallic patch**, I knew it would be perfect on a black background.

1. Position the anchor patch near the top. Attach the patch by hand, sewing it with gold thread, or use fabric glue. If the patch is an iron-on, follow the manufacturer's instructions for adhering it .

2. Add extra embellishments by adding iron-on star studs to the sleeves and around the patch design. You might need to use a pressing cloth over the patches.

 # Little Flirt

Use **rhinestone iron-ons to spell out words:** the flirtier, the better. A coordinating ruffle trim sewn around the sleeves accentuates the sparkle.

1. Center the iron-on in the desired position. Follow the manufacturer's instructions for adhering it to the fabric.

2. Hand sew the ruffle trim around the shoulder seams.

TIP: For extra glitz, sew trim or ribbon to the neckline.

Variation
Paris

Mix it up and match it. When using an iron-on with multi-colors, choose one of the colors in the design to dye the suit.

Queen Bee

Every new mom and dad knows who the real queen bee of the household is.
Now it's time to let everyone else in on it with **metallic iron-on letters**.

1. Attach the iron-on bee following the manufacturer's instructions for adhering it to the fabric. For more information on iron-ons, visit chapter 6.

2. Line up the letters across the top of the bee. To get the gentle curve in the word, use the edge of a plate or other round object as a guideline. Follow the manufacturer's instructions for adhering the letters to the fabric.

  # Baby Blossoms

Most shops stock **loose rhinestones** in hundreds of colors and sizes; you have even more options online. When it comes to baby fashions, small rhinestones are the safest bet.

1. Slide a piece of waxed paper inside the suit to prevent paint and glue from seeping through to the other side.

2. Use a foam paintbrush to apply a coat of metallic purple brush-on fabric paint to a foam floral stamp. Apply the stamp in the desired position. Stamp more layers of flowers until you've covered a large area. Allow the paint to dry. Heat set following the manufacturer's instructions.

3. Place a small amount of gem glue on a piece of waxed paper, dip the head of a straight pin into the glue, and dot the glue in the center of the flowers. Attach the rhinestones and allow to dry.

Variation
Blue Beauty

Try using Aurora Borealis rhinestones. They have an outer coating that produces an iridescent effect and tend to reflect whatever color is near the stone, in this case blue accents.

Bling

If a string of pearls goes with anything, why not a snapsuit? The design, created with **pearlescent fabric paint**, is based on my dream necklace—a giant diamond with south sea pearls!

1. Slide a piece of waxed paper inside the suit to prevent paint from seeping through to the other side.

2. Paint a circle at the top center using silver glitter dimensional fabric paint.

3. To make the pearls, you'll apply pearl white dimensional fabric paint directly from the bottle. Next to the circle of glitter paint, and working with the paint bottle in an upright position, squeeze the bottle to form a drop about the size of a small pearl. Keep adding drops to make the pearl necklace. Allow the paint to dry 48 hours before laundering.

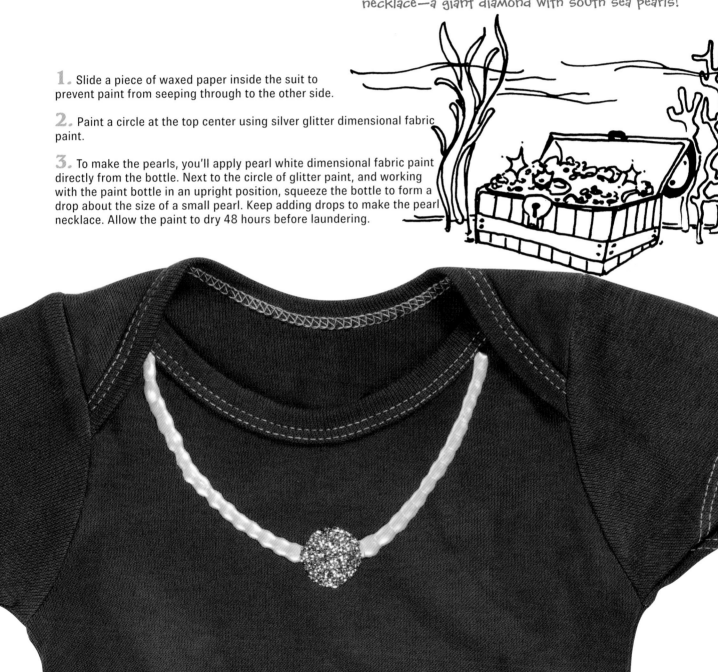

18kt Girl

Let everyone know diamonds are your girl's best friend with a little **gold metallic paint**. You could also use colors to match the baby's birthstone.

1. Slide a piece of waxed paper inside a suit to prevent paint from seeping through to the other side.

2. Use a foam paintbrush to apply gold metallic brush-on fabric paint to a foam diamond ring stamp. Stamp in the top center, and allow the paint to dry. Heat set the paint following the manufacturer's instruction.

3. Use gold glitter brush-on fabric paint to add sparkling highlights to the diamond.

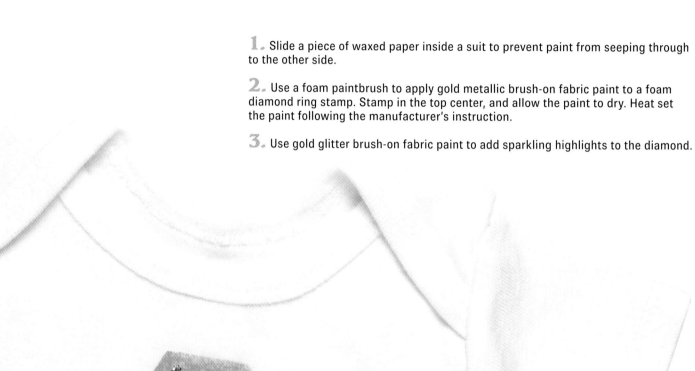

Poppy 8 7

Swirling a wide, soft-bristled **paintbrush** over a print **appliqué** delivers touches of glittery highlights to the design.

1. Make an appliqué by cutting a motif from a floral print fabric. Sew it to the front. For more information on appliqué, visit chapter 3.

2. Slide a piece of waxed paper inside the suit to prevent paint from seeping through to the other side. Load the paintbrush with gold glitter brush-on fabric paint. Tap the brush on a piece of waxed paper to remove any excess paint. You want the brush to be fairly dry. Highlight the flowers by swirling the paint onto the floral fabric. Allow to dry.

TIP: Create a multi-glittered look by loading the brush with different colors of glitter paint prior to painting.

 # Rodeo Queen

Let your little darlin' show some love for the wide open spaces of the Lone Star State. Using **dimensional glitter fabric paint** to outline an iron-on is a great way to highlight the design.

1. Attach a Texas iron-on to the front. Follow the manufacturer's instructions for adhering it to the fabric. Do the same for the iron-on star studs.

2. Slide a piece of waxed paper inside the snapsuit to prevent paint from seeping through to the other side. Use glitter dimensional paint to trace around the outer edge of the iron-on. Allow the paint to dry 48 hours before laundering.

Evel K

Be a little daredevil. **Iron-on foil transfers** are available in premade designs, or you can buy the material in sheets for making your own creations.

1. Tie-dye a snapsuit in a dark color with a white stripe down the center (page 14). For more on dyeing, visit chapter 1.

2. Cut a strip of premade iron-on foil stars. Attach the strip following the manufacturer's instructions for attaching it to the fabric. Once cool, gently buff the edges of the stars with a fine emery board to distress them.

Variation
Smooch

Kissy, kissy. A big and bold foil transfer design looks great on a little snapsuit.

 Rock Star

Hey, glitz and glam aren't just for the girls! Use a touch of **glitter and dimensional paint** for a design that's rough and tumble.

1. Look for guitar and flame stencils that will fit on a snapsuit. Slide a piece of waxed paper inside the suit to prevent paint from seeping through to the other side.

2. Use a stencil brush and brush-on fabric paint in black and red to stencil the guitar and flames onto the fabric. Make sure to position the guitar to leave room for the lettering.

3. Use red glitter and shiny black dimensional fabric paint to highlight the stenciled design. Allow the paint to dry. Heat set following the manufacturer's instructions.

4. Position iron-on letters to spell STAR above the guitar. Have the word follow the curve of the neckline. Follow the manufacturer's instructions for adhering them to the fabric.

Variation
Dream Speedway

A little bling goes a long way when incorporated into a guy's design. The iron-on studs serve as the roadway for the stenciled design.

Chapter 10
Holidays

Holidays and celebrations are especially fun days for dressing a little one in a customized snapsuit. You'll show off your holiday spirit *and* get lots of ooohhhs and awwwws from grandmothers and aunts.

Celebrate in Style

The projects in this chapter focus on the main calendar holidays and family celebrations, such as Christmas, birthdays, Valentine's Day, and Halloween. All the designs feature simple techniques from previous chapters, so you'll be able to whip them up in a flash.

Of course, you can create a design for any holiday from Chinese New Year to Groundhog Day. And don't forget National Hug Day! Have fun using what you've already learned as inspiration for creating your own themes.

Celebrating Firsts

Family celebrations are not just holidays on the calendar. With a newborn in the house, it seems as though every movement they make becomes something to celebrate and cheer—first time crawling, first words, and the first bite of real food. If you photograph it or write about it in the baby book, why not make a suit to commemorate it? There's no better way to announce to the world how proud you are of your little kiddo.

Q & A

Q: *Where can I get holiday design ideas?*

A: There are almost too many to count. Check out vintage greeting cards, wrapping paper, books of clip art, and holiday fabrics for inspiring patterns and pictures. A quick trip to a stationery store, bookseller, or fabric shop should get the creative juices flowing. Or search online for a world of possibilities.

Let Me Eat Cake

Celebrate the all-important first birthday with the perfect design complete with a **cake stencil.** But be warned, this snapsuit will likely stay clean only a few minutes until it's decorated with real cake.

1. Copy the template on page 171, and cut it out. Use it to cut out a cake shape from a kitchen sponge to make a stamp. Use a foam paintbrush to apply brush-on fabric paint to one side of the stamp. Press the stamp onto the center front. Allow the paint to dry, then heat set following the manufacturer's instructions.

2. Attach paper-backed fusible web to the wrong side of a faux suede fabric. Cut out the frosting from the template. Trace it on the back of the webbing, and cut it out. Position it at the top of the stamped cake. Remove the paper backing, and follow the manufacturer's instructions for adhering it to the fabric. Sew the appliqué around the edges to secure it.

3. Sew or glue floral embroidered trim to the edge of the cake as a decorative finish of frosting. Add a strip of rickrack trim down the center of the cake. Sew a scrap of ribbon at the top of the cake for the candle. Draw a flame using gold glitter dimensional fabric paint.

TIP: Customize the color of the cake to your liking. Use any of the appliqué techniques in the book. For more on appliqué, visit chapter 3.

Variation

I am ONE!

This #1 patch is the perfect way to show off a baby's age. If the patch is an iron-on, follow the manufacturer's instructions for adhering it to the fabric. If not, use fabric glue or hand stitch to attach. For an iron-on or glued patch, hand sew around the edge for extra security.

 # Wake Me at Midnight

Even though you know most newborns will be sound asleep when the clock strikes 12, let them celebrate in quiet style from their crib. They'll be snug as a bug in this party-ready suit with **iron-on letters.**

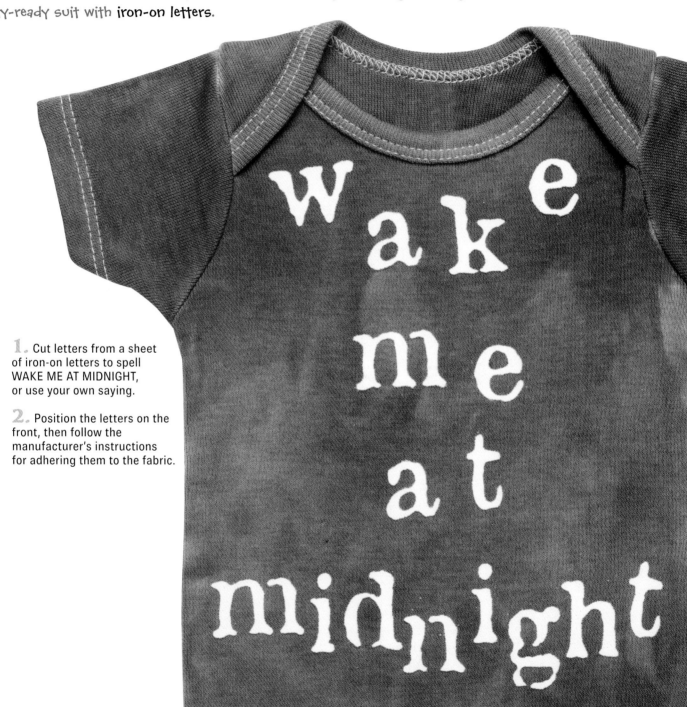

1. Cut letters from a sheet of iron-on letters to spell WAKE ME AT MIDNIGHT, or use your own saying.

2. Position the letters on the front, then follow the manufacturer's instructions for adhering them to the fabric.

I Heart You!

Valentine's Day is all about love—and shiny stuff. This red-hot
heart rhinestone design looks perfectly pretty on a pink snapsuit.

1. Center iron-on rhinestones
to make a heart in the desired
position.

2. Follow the manufacturer's
instructions for adhering them
to the fabric.

Variation
My Deer

Vintage Valentine cards are great for making
inkjet transfers. They have such a nostalgic
look and are almost always perfectly sized
for snapsuits. For more information on inkjet
transfers, visit chapter 6.

Lucky Me

Babies might not be old enough for corned beef and cabbage and green beer, but they're certainly special enough to celebrate the luck of the Irish. This green suit with **stenciled metallic letters** should ensure a pinch-free St. Patty's day.

1. Find an Irish-themed stencil or make your own by combining letter stencils with a clover stencil. Align the stencil or stencils on the front. Use low-tack tape to secure them to the fabric.

2. Dab a stencil brush in either metallic green or gold brush-on fabric paint. Tap off the excess; you want to work with the brush semi-dry. Working with up and down strokes, tap the brush over the stencil. Don't brush side to side.

3. Allow the paint to dry, remove the stencil, and heat set the paint following the manufacturer's instructions.

TIP: For a different look, use one color of paint first, then highlight it with the other color.

Silly Rabbit

Just like Peter Cottontail, babies are soft and cuddly. And just like this silly **rabbit appliqué,** they can be cute and funny on Easter or any day of the year.

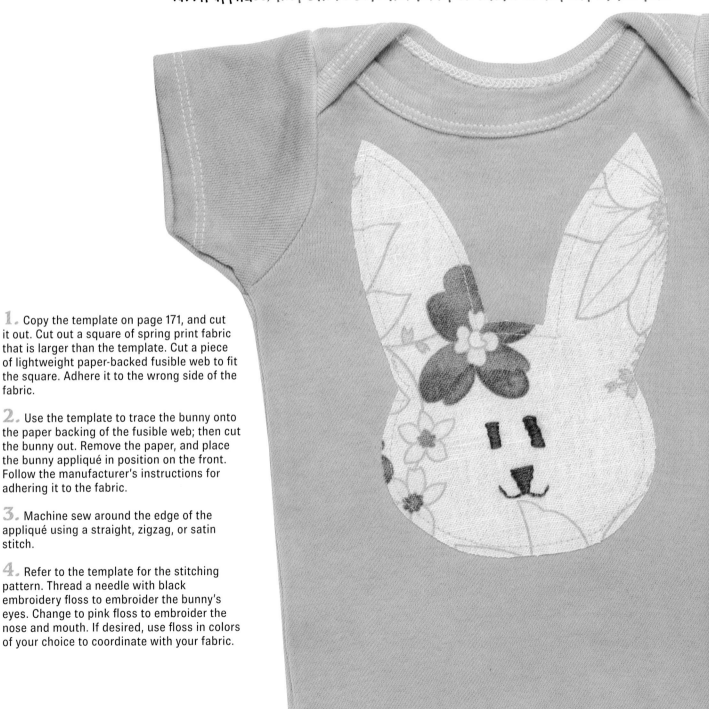

1. Copy the template on page 171, and cut it out. Cut out a square of spring print fabric that is larger than the template. Cut a piece of lightweight paper-backed fusible web to fit the square. Adhere it to the wrong side of the fabric.

2. Use the template to trace the bunny onto the paper backing of the fusible web; then cut the bunny out. Remove the paper, and place the bunny appliqué in position on the front. Follow the manufacturer's instructions for adhering it to the fabric.

3. Machine sew around the edge of the appliqué using a straight, zigzag, or satin stitch.

4. Refer to the template for the stitching pattern. Thread a needle with black embroidery floss to embroider the bunny's eyes. Change to pink floss to embroider the nose and mouth. If desired, use floss in colors of your choice to coordinate with your fabric.

  # Mini Me

Surprise mom or dad with a snapsuit designed for their special day. You could spell out a humorous saying with a **homemade stencil.**

1. Create and print out the words Mini Me from the computer using a bold, fun font of your choice. Make a stencil from self-stick shelf liner using the printout. If you've forgotten how, see page 32 for step-by-step instructions

2. Slide a piece of waxed paper inside the suit. Position the stencil on the front, and press the edges to secure it to the fabric.

3. Using brush-on fabric paint and a foam paintbrush, paint the stencil in an up-and-down motion. Before you begin painting, remove any excess paint from the brush; you want to work with it semi-dry.

4. Allow the paint to dry, remove the stencil, and heat set the paint following the manufacturer's instructions.

Variation
My Mommy Is Cool

Your little babe might be too young for a sailor tat, but not a tattoo patch. This cool MOM patch was found at a fabric store for way less than the cost (and pain) of a real tattoo.

It's all about red, white, and blue! Double dip the suit and then add **embroidered fireworks** for extra sparkle and pop.

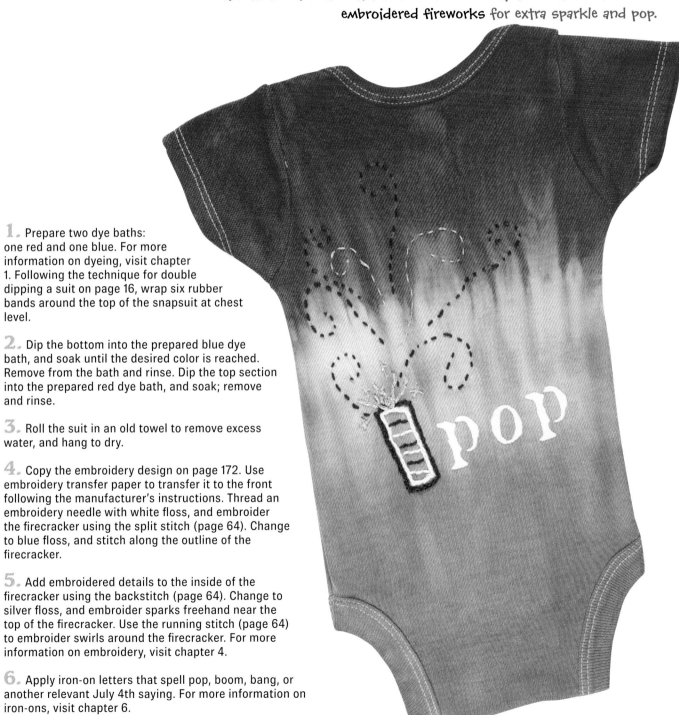

1. Prepare two dye baths: one red and one blue. For more information on dyeing, visit chapter 1. Following the technique for double dipping a suit on page 16, wrap six rubber bands around the top of the snapsuit at chest level.

2. Dip the bottom into the prepared blue dye bath, and soak until the desired color is reached. Remove from the bath and rinse. Dip the top section into the prepared red dye bath, and soak; remove and rinse.

3. Roll the suit in an old towel to remove excess water, and hang to dry.

4. Copy the embroidery design on page 172. Use embroidery transfer paper to transfer it to the front following the manufacturer's instructions. Thread an embroidery needle with white floss, and embroider the firecracker using the split stitch (page 64). Change to blue floss, and stitch along the outline of the firecracker.

5. Add embroidered details to the inside of the firecracker using the backstitch (page 64). Change to silver floss, and embroider sparks freehand near the top of the firecracker. Use the running stitch (page 64) to embroider swirls around the firecracker. For more information on embroidery, visit chapter 4.

6. Apply iron-on letters that spell pop, boom, bang, or another relevant July 4th saying. For more information on iron-ons, visit chapter 6.

Variation
Little Firecracker

Look for images of firecracker labels to make inkjet transfers. You can find them in clip art books or online. Vintage labels date back to the 1920s and feature everything from panda bears and tigers to robots and rockets. For more information on inkjet transfers, visit chapter 6.

Get ready to trick or treat. Start with an orange suit, then see how many different jack-o'-lantern faces you can make from black **felt appliqués**.

1. Copy the template on page 172. Use it to cut black felt triangles for the eyes and nose and a big toothy smile for the mouth. Or use your own design from a favorite jack-o'-lantern.

2. Thread a needle with yellow embroidery floss. Use the running stitch (page 64) to attach the felt to the snapsuit.

3. Hand stitch green trim around the neckline.

TIP: If you want to go a bit more Goth, consider using a cutout skull, bat, or witch.

  # My Sister Is an Artist

Enlist big brother or sister to give you a hand in making the drawing for the **crayon transfer.** You'll be thankful you did. Kids love to help, and it's super easy on you.

1. Trace the hand of a child on white paper using fabric transfer crayons. Add, or have the child draw, the other elements to define the turkey. Press hard while drawing. Brush away any loose specks of wax. For more on transfer fabric crayons, visit chapter 6.

2. Place a piece of white paper inside the suit to prevent the color from seeping to the other side.

3. Place the drawing facedown in the desired position on the front. Press the paper with a hot iron, no steam. Press and hold as you iron for one to two minutes. Try not to move the paper as you press.

4. Carefully remove the paper, launder in cold water, and hang to dry.

Santa Baby

When I was growing up, my mom dressed me and my siblings in matching holiday sweaters. I can only imagine how thrilled she'd be to see her little grandbaby dressed in a Santa snapsuit decorated with a **print fabric appliqué.**

1. Cut out a motif from a Santa-themed print fabric. Leave at least a ¹/₂-inch (1.3 cm) allowance around the edges.

2. Cut a piece of lightweight paper-backed fusible web to fit the cutout. Follow the manufacturer's instructions to fuse the webbing to the wrong side of the fabric.

3. Cut out the motif by cutting away the allowance you left in step 1. Remove the paper backing, and place the appliqué in the desired position. Follow the manufacturer's instructions to fuse the appliqué to the front. If needed, use a pressing cloth over the motif.

4. Machine sew around the edges of the appliqué using a straight, zigzag, or satin stitch (page 45).

5. Use fabric glue to attach a pom-pom to the Santa hat. After the glue has dried, hand sew the pom-pom for extra security.

Variation
Spin Baby

Tie-dye a circle in the center of a suit to simulate the spinning dreidel. For more information on tie-dyeing circles, see page 20. Make the dreidel from felt, and sew it to the suit. Embellish the dreidel appliqué by embroidering it with the Hebrew letter "Hei."

fashion
meets
tiny
toes

Chapter 11

Throwing a Snappy Baby Shower

Forget those stuffy, frilly baby showers of the past, and get ready to wow the mom-to-be and her friends with a creative baby shower that's all about snapsuits. From themed invites to fab gloves for dyeing, your guests will enjoy creating an outfit for the newborn using the designs in this book for ideas and inspiration.

Invitations & Paper Goods

Nothing sets the mood for a crafty party like a handmade invitation. Use the paper snapsuit-shaped template (page 173) to create many different styles of themed invitations. The same template can be used to make guest cards that can be signed at the party and later used in a scrapbook for the baby.

Decorations

Hanging a celebration banner—especially the snappy kind—makes a sweet, festive, and totally crafty statement. Create a simple banner like this one with punched paper ovals and letter stickers. If you're sending your guests home with a favor, use the snapsuit template to make a cute gift tag that can double as decoration.

Snapsuit-Decorating Station

And now for the main event: let the snapsuit creativity commence. Start with an organized decorating station; one large worktable or several smaller tables will work nicely. In the center of the table, place a colorful collection of tools and supplies: fabric paints, markers, foam stamps, scissors, embroidery floss, and fabric.

You will need at least one plain pre-washed suit per guest. Purchase them in various sizes so the new baby will have a year's worth of original looks. For iron-on designs, set up an ironing board and iron. And for stitched creations, designate a sewing table away from the paints.

If your guests will be dyeing snapsuits, pre-make the dye baths in buckets. Help partygoers stay clean with a super-cute apron (made with fusible web, the snapsuit template, and a little bit of stitching) and some fabulous glammed-up gloves. To dry the suits, toss them in the dryer with a few rag towels, or set up a clothesline outside; that way, guests can admire their work.

Sweet Tweet

Whale of a Good Time

Angel Baby

Play Ball Enlarge 125%

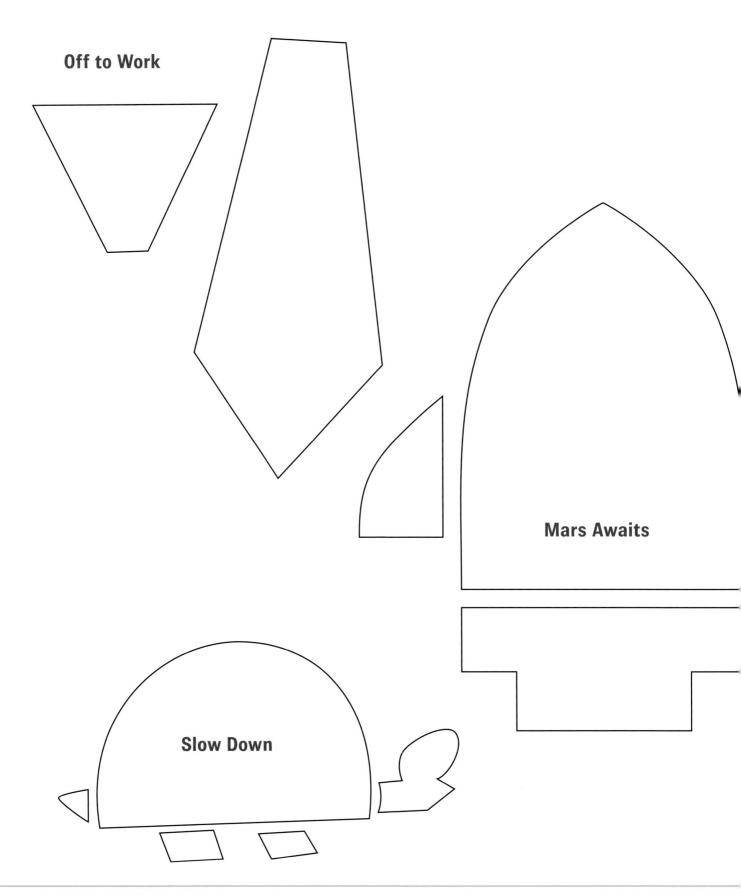

Off to Work

Mars Awaits

Slow Down

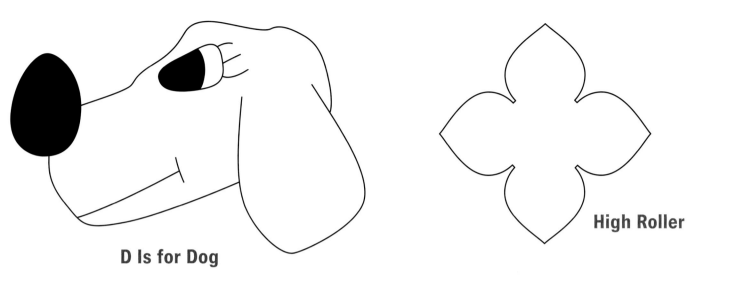

D Is for Dog

High Roller

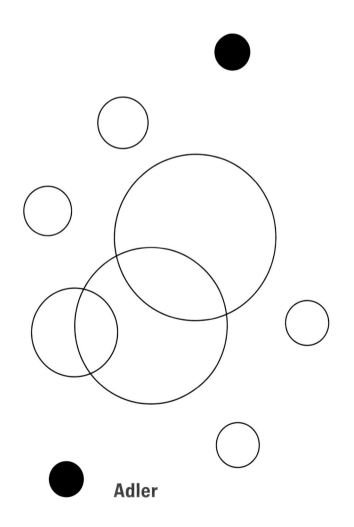

Adler

Tiki Time

Tattooed

Tulips

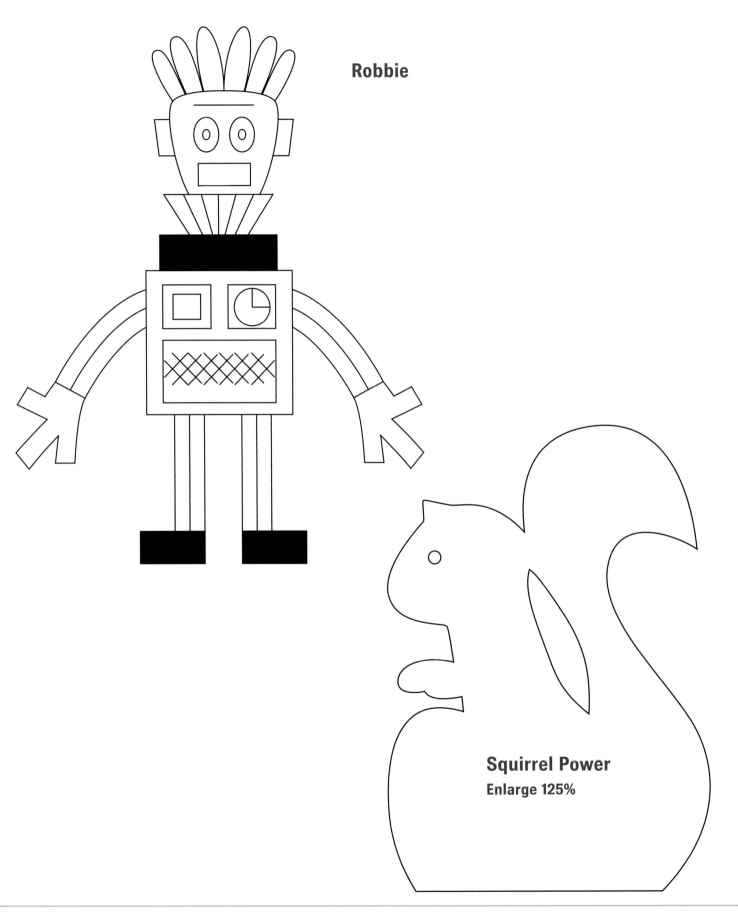

Robbie

Squirrel Power
Enlarge 125%

Sunday Drive

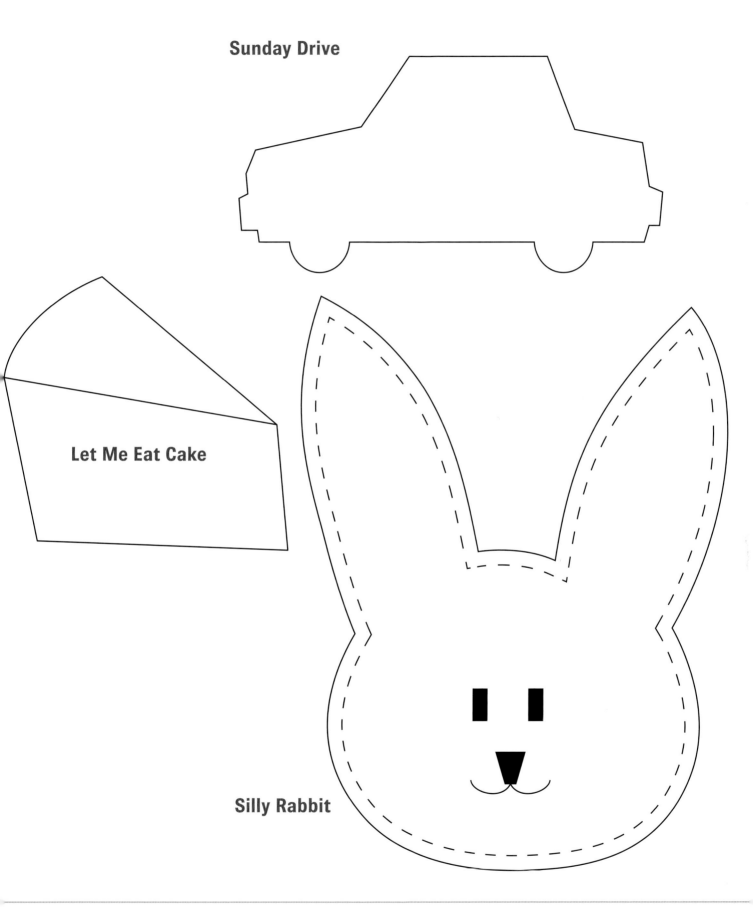

Let Me Eat Cake

Silly Rabbit

My First Fourth

Little Punkin

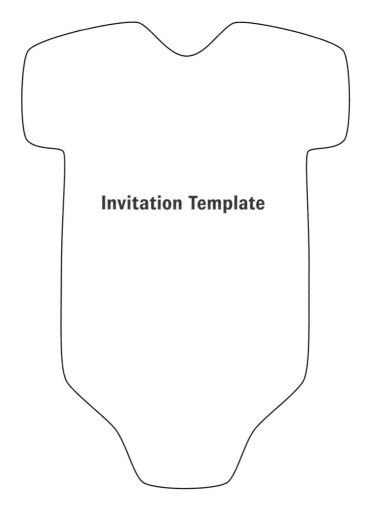

Invitation Template

About the Author

D.I.Y. guru, Cathie Filian, brings a fresh approach to creative living with her outside-the-box ideas for crafts, recipes, and home decor. She is a little bit country, a little bit rock-n-roll, and all original.

Cathie created, produces, and co-hosts the popular lifestyle shows *Creative Juice* and *Witch Crafts* on HGTV & DIY Network. She was nominated for an Emmy for Outstanding Lifestyle Host for her work on *Creative Juice* and was nominated for a second Emmy for Outstanding Lifestyle Host Program for her work on *Witch Crafts*.

Her first book, *Creative Juice: 45 Re-Crafting Projects*, is filled with fun and funky recycling craft ideas that can be made for pennies. Her second book, *Bow Wow WOW! Fetching Costumes for Your Fabulous Dog*, is full of patterns and ideas for creating pet fashions. Both were published by Lark Books.

Cathie is the national spokesperson for Plaid Enterprises, one of the largest manufacturers of art and craft products in the United States,

In addition to books, Cathie writes "Home Hobbies", a syndicated newspaper column for United Features and a Lifestyle Blog. She also contributes to national shelter publications such as *Life* magazine, *Real Simple*, *Redbook*, and many others.

Cathie grew up in the Midwest and has been getting crafty for as long as she can remember. She began sewing when she was eight and her love of stitching followed her all the way to college, where she studied Textile Science and Fashion Design at Ohio State University. In her senior year she was awarded the Outstanding Senior Design Award.

Before *Creative Juice*, Cathie worked in the film business creating costumes for such films as *Rushmore*, *Twister*, *Heartbreakers*, and *Vanilla Sky*. Cathie lives in Los Angeles with her husband, Eddie, and their dog, Max.

Visit her blog (www.cathiefilian.com) or website (www. cathieandsteve.com).

Acknowledgments

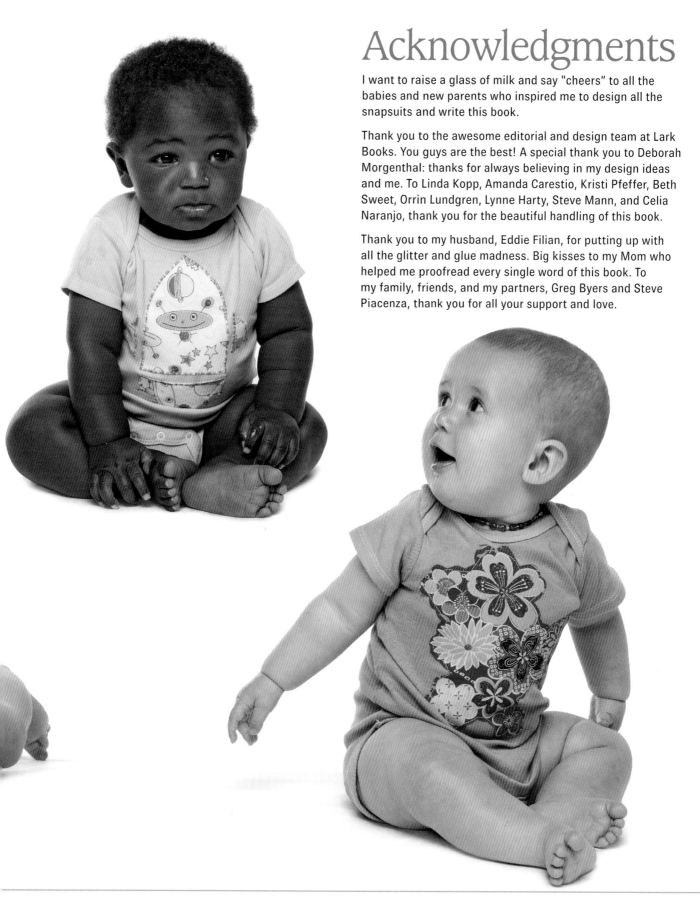

I want to raise a glass of milk and say "cheers" to all the babies and new parents who inspired me to design all the snapsuits and write this book.

Thank you to the awesome editorial and design team at Lark Books. You guys are the best! A special thank you to Deborah Morgenthal: thanks for always believing in my design ideas and me. To Linda Kopp, Amanda Carestio, Kristi Pfeffer, Beth Sweet, Orrin Lundgren, Lynne Harty, Steve Mann, and Celia Naranjo, thank you for the beautiful handling of this book.

Thank you to my husband, Eddie Filian, for putting up with all the glitter and glue madness. Big kisses to my Mom who helped me proofread every single word of this book. To my family, friends, and my partners, Greg Byers and Steve Piacenza, thank you for all your support and love.

Index